POTAWATOMI INDIANS OF MICHIGAN
1843-1904

Including some
Ottawa and Chippewa
1843-1866
and
Potawatomi of Indiana
1869 and 1885

Raymond C. Lantz

HERITAGE BOOKS
2007

HERITAGE BOOKS

AN IMPRINT OF HERITAGE BOOKS, INC.

Books, CDs, and more—Worldwide

For our listing of thousands of titles see our website
at
www.HeritageBooks.com

Published 2007 by
HERITAGE BOOKS, INC.
Publishing Division
65 East Main Street
Westminster, Maryland 21157-5026

Copyright © 1992 Raymond C. Lantz

Other books by the author:

Lantz-Crossley: An Experience in Genealogy
Ottawa and Chippewa Indians of Michigan, 1855-1868
Ottawa and Chippewa Indians of Michigan, 1870-1909
Seminole Indians of Florida: 1850-1874
Seminole Indians of Florida: 1875-1879

International Standard Book Number: 978-1-55613-619-6

Table of Contents

Foreword

All the information contained in this book has been transcribed from the records of the Department of Interior, Bureau of Indian Affairs Records which are a part of the holdings of the National Archives in Washington D.C. These annuity rolls and censuses were taken to determine the eligibility of persons of Indian descent to receive payment of monies as the result of U.S. Congressional Legislation and Treaties signed between the Indian tribes and the government of the United States.

1843 thru 1866 Annuity Rolls for the Ottawa, Chippewa and Potawatomi of Michigan, Mackinac Agency, contain name, number of men/number of women/number of children/ total in family, annuity ammount and current roll number. These rolls were taken for the purpose of payment of money in compliance with the Treaty of July 29, 1829 and the supplimental treaty of September 26, 1833. The following give the dates that the respective rolls were taken:

```
1843 - November 2, 1843, Note: no roll number #25
              and roll number #27 used twice
1844 - October 25, 1844
1845 - October 17, 1845
1846 - November 21, 1846
1847 - November 27, 1847
1848 - November 28, 1848
1849 - October 29, 1849
1850 - December 18, 1850
1851 - November 4, 1851
1852 - October 26, 1852
1853 - January 19, 1854
1854 - December 26, 1854
1855 - December 11, 1855
1856 - December 10, 1856, Note: roll number #26
              used twice and roll number #60 not used
1857 - January 21, 1858
1858 - December 31, 1858
1859 - February 14, 1860, Note: roll #35 not used
1860 - December 13, 1860
1861 - December 31, 1861
1862 - December 26, 1862
1863 - December 26, 1863
1864 - December 21, 1864
1865 - December 30, 1865
1866 - November 21, 1866
```

1861 4th quarter Annuity Roll for the Potawatomi of Huron was taken on December 31, 1861 and was for the purpose of payment of monies as the result of a treaty signed November 17, 1807. This section contains name, number of men/number of women/number of children/total in household, amount of annuity and current roll number.

1869 3rd quarter Annuity Roll for the Potawatomi of Indiana and Michigan was taken on July 31, 1869. This section contains name, number of men/number of women/number of children/total in household, amount of annuity and current roll number. The compiler of this book feels that the persons tasked to compile this document were not overly concerned with its accuracy. The original document bears obvious mistakes in the enumeration numbers such as enumerating a woman in the men column and vice versa and many families grouped in the children column. Also it would appear that many of the indian name spellings are not phonetically correct.

1874 thru 1876 Annuity Rolls for the Potawatomi of Huron contain name, number of men/number of women/number of children/total in household, annuity amount and current roll number, remarks when applicable. The following give the dates that the respective rolls were taken:

> 1874 - February 25, 1875 (taken in 1875 but clearly states for the year 1874)
> 1875 - November 30, 1875 (refered to as 4th quarter roll but states for entire year)
> 1876 - December 13, 1876

1877 thru 1883 Annuity Rolls for the Potawatomi of Huron contain name, relationship, age, sex, current roll number, annuity amount and remarks when applicable. The following give the dates that the respective rolls were taken:

> 1877 - December 4, 1877
> 1878 - November 26, 1878
> 1879 - November 25, 1879
> 1880 - November 24, 1880 (refered to as 4th quarter roll but states for entire year)
> 1882 - April 25, 1882 (refered to as the 2nd quarter but states for entire year)
> 1883 - April 26 & May 4 1883 (refered to as 2nd quarter roll but states for entire year)

1884 thru 1889 Annuity Rolls for the Potawatomi of Huron contain name, relationship, age, sex, previous roll number/current roll number, annuity amount and remarks when applicable. These rolls were for the purpose of payment of monies as the result of a treaty signed November 17, 1808, except 1889 1st quarter for treaty of August 7, 1868. The following give the dates that the respective rolls were taken:

1884 - April 29, 1884
1885 - May 1, 1885
1886 - May 11, 1886
1887 - February 1887
1888 - May 1888
1889 1st Qtr. - March 21, 1889
1889 - March 21, 1889

1895 Census of August 5th of the Potawatomi of Indiana and Michigan states that these Indians were last paid in 1866 and were enumerated by John W. Cadman, U.S. Indian Inspector. The census is well known as the "Cadman Roll" and is refered to in the Bureau of Indian Affairs' manual as "Cadman payment roll of 1896." Information given in this section is name, relationship, sex, age, 1866 roll number/current roll number, residence and remarks when applicable.

1904 Census of the Potawatomi of Michigan was taken on October 21, 1904 by S. L. Taggart, Special U.S. Indian Agent. This roll was taken as the result of Indian Appropriation Act of April 21, 1904 (33 stats., 210). The roll is commonly refered to as the "Taggart Roll" and is refered to in the Bureau of Indian Affairs' manual as the "Taggart census roll of 1904."

Raymond C. Lantz

PRINCIPAL ABBREVIATIONS USED

Auth	-	Authority
b	-	born
bro	-	brother
d	-	died
dau	-	daughter
dec'd	-	deceased
f	-	female
gdau	-	granddaughter
ggd	-	great granddaughter
gson	-	grandson
hbro	-	half brother
hsis	-	half sister
husb	-	husband
Jr	-	Junior
m	-	male
mo	-	month
neph	-	nephew
Rem	-	remarks
Res	-	residence
sdau	-	stepdaughter
sis	-	sister
Sr	-	Senior
sson	-	stepson
wk	-	week

1843 ANNUITY ROLL FOR YEAR
CHIPPEWA, OTTAWA & POTAWATOMI OF MICHIGAN

PAW PAW & POKAGON BANDS

PEEN DUN WAW (Chief) 1/1/7/9 $56.43 #1
SUN A GO WAW (Chief) 1/1/5/7 $43.89 #2
PEE PEE AW (Chief) 1/0/0/1 $6.27 #3
WAW GAUK SHIG 1/1/6/8 $50.16 #4
CAW GEES THAY 1/1/7/9 $56.43 #5
SEE THONE 1/1/7/9 $56.43 #6
WAW BEE MANIDO 1/1/5/7 $43.89 #7
CAW ME NO THO AH 1/1/6/8 $50.16 #8
NAY WODGE A GEE A GEEZHICK 1/1/1/3 $18.81 #9
POKAGON (Chief) 1/1/0/2 $12.54 #10
KAY THACE 1/1/2/4 $25.08 #11
WEE ZHO 1/1/1/3 $18.81 #12
NIS SEE GAY THAY 1/1/0/2 $12.54 #13
CAW BAY MUS SAY 1/1/4/6 $37.62 #14
A MO NO 1/1/1/3 $18.81 #15
SKUS ZHEESH 1/1/1/3 $18.81 #16
SHANG AW BE 1/1/1/3 $18.81 #17
NAW WAY QUAW AW 1/1/1/3 $18.81 #18
MO CO BEE QUAY 0/1/1/2 $12.54 #19
TUSH QUAY GEEZHICK O QUAY 0/1/5/6 $37.62 #20
DUN ACE 1/1/4/6 $37.62 #21
PAY MAW MEE 1/1/2/4 $25.08 #22
SHAY GO NAY BEE 1/1/5/7 $43.89 #23
WAIN GEE CEE AW 1/1/3/5 $31.35 #24
SAW GEE 1/1/7/9 $56.43 #26
SHAW BO TEESE 1/1/1/3 $18.81 #27
E DO WAY GEEZHICK 1/1/7/9 $56.43 #27
NAY IN O QUAY 0/1/2/3 $18.81 #28
AW SUG 1/1/2/4 $25.08 #29
WAW BUN O QUAY 1/1/4/6 $37.62 #30
AIN WEE 1/1/5/7 $43.89 #31
WAUB MO AY 1/1/7/9 $56.43 #32
TAW GAW 1/1/7/9 $56.43 #33
CO THAY QUAY 0/1/2/3 $18.81 #34
OH TUCK WEE 1/0/0/1 $6.27 #35
NAW ZHEE WAY QUAY 0/1/1/2 $12.54 #36
WAY SAW WAY SHUCK 1/1/4/6 $37.62 #37
PAY SHE WAY 1/1/3/5 $31.35 #38
NAUD WAEE 1/1/1/3 $18.81 #39
PAY MAW MEE 1/1/1/3 $18.81 #40
ME NIS IN O QUAY 0/1/4/5 $31.35 #41

NAUD DAY WAY SEE PEE BAND

MO GWAW GO (Chief) 1/1/1/3 $18.81 #1

1

PAIM THUB BEE 1/1/5/7 $43.89 #2
WAY MIT TAY GO SHEE QUAY 0/1/2/3 $18.81 #3
BAY WAW NEE 1/1/5/7 $43.89 #4
MAIN JAW WON O QUAY 0/1/4/5 $31.35 #5
THO CUB AW 1/1/3/5 $31.35 #6
MEN O QUET 1/1/3/5 $31.35 #7
MEN DO KAY 1/0/0/1 $6.27 #8
MAY THAY O MAIG 1/1/0/2 $12.54 #9
WAY SAW AW ZHICK 1/1/3/5 $31.35 #10
WAW SOM O QUAY 0/1/1/2 $12.54 #11
WAW KAY OS IN O QUAY 0/1/0/1 $6.27 #12

1844 ANNUITY ROLL FOR YEAR
CHIPPEWA, OTTAWA & POTAWATOMI OF MICHIGAN

PAW PAW BAND

PEEN DUN WAUN (1st Chief) 1/1/9/11 $64.90 #1
SUN A GO WAW (Chief) 1/1/8/10 $59.00 #2
PEE PEE AW (Chief) 1/1/4/6 $35.40 #3
WAW GANG SHIG 1/1/5/7 $41.30 #4
CAW GEESH THAY 1/1/7/9 $53.10 #5
SEE THONE 1/1/5/7 $41.30 #6
WAW BE MANIDO 1/1/3/5 $29.50 #7
CAW ME NO THAY AH 1/1/7/9 $53.10 #8
NAY WODGE A GEEZHICK 1/1/1/3 $17.70 #9
POKAGON (Chief) 1/1/2/4 $23.60 #10
KAY THACE 1/1/3/5 $29.50 #11
WEE ZO 1/1/2/4 $23.60 #12
A MO NO 1/1/2/4 $23.60 #13
SKEES ZHEESH 1/1/2/4 $23.60 #14
CHAW GAW BE 1/1/0/2 $11.80 #15
NAW WAY QUAY AW 1/1/1/3 $17.70 #16
MO CO BEE QUAY 1/1/0/2 $11.80 #17
SQUAY GEEZHICK OQUAY 0/1/4/5 $29.50 #18
DUN NACE 1/1/3/5 $29.50 #19
PAY MAW MEE 1/1/1/3 $17.70 #20
MONG GO QUAY 0/1/3/4 $23.60 #21
WAIN GEE SEE AW 1/1/4/6 $35.40 #22
SAY GEE 1/1/5/7 $41.30 #23
SHAW BO TEESE 1/1/1/3 $17.70 #24
E DO WAY GEEZHICK 1/1/4/6 $36.40 #25
NAY IN O QUAY 0/1/2/3 $17.70 #26
AW SUG 0/1/4/5 $29.50 #27
WAW BUN O QUAY 0/1/4/5 $29.50 #28
AIN WEE 1/1/6/8 $47.20 #29
WAW BE MO WAY 1/1/3/5 $29.50 #30
TAW GAW 1/1/8/10 $59.00 #31
CO THAY QUAY 0/1/0/1 $5.90 #32

2

OH TUCK WIN 1/0/0/1 $5.90 #33
NAW ZHEE WAY QUAY 0/1/1/2 $11.80 #34
WAY SUN WAY SHUCK 1/1/0/2 $11.80 #35
NAUD DO WACE 1/1/1/3 $17.70 #36
PAY MAW MEE 1/1/3/5 $29.50 #37
ME NIS IN O QUAY 0/1/4/5 $29.50 #38
KAY KAKE 1/1/2/4 $23.60 #39
CAW GAY AW MAIG 1/1/1/3 $17.70 #40
KIN NEESE QUAY 0/1/2/3 $17.70 #41
ON NAY GISH 1/1/2/4 $23.60 #42
O SKIN NEE WAY 1/1/2/4 $23.60 #43
BERTRAND, Mrs. 0/1/0/1 $5.90 #44

NAUD DAY WAY SEE PEE BAND

MO GWAW GO (Chief) 1/1/3/5 $29.50 #1
PAIM THUB BEE 1/1/4/6 $35.40 #2
WAY MIT THAY GO ZHEE QUAY 0/1/4/5 $29.50 #3
MAW CHEE AN O QUAY 0/1/3/4 $23.60 #4
CHEE GON NAY QUAY SEE 1/1/0/2 $11.80 #5
SEE BEE QUAY 0/1/0/1 $5.90 #6
MEN DO KAY 1/0/0/1 $5.90 #7
PIN ISH AW WAY 1/1/6/8 $47.20 #8
WAY SAW WAY SHICK 1/1/2/4 $23.60 #9
KEE WOS IN O QUAY 0/1/0/1 $5.90 #10
PAIM THUB BEE 1/1/4/6 $35.40 #11
MAY THAY O MAIG 1/1/1/3 $17.70 #12
AU NIM A KEE QUAY 0/1/1/2 $11.80 #13
NUCK QUOT 1/1/2/4 $23.60 #14
WAY KEE TAY ZEE 1/1/0/2 #15
MAY E TAY O QUOT 1/1/1/3 $17.70 #16
WAY SEE BAH 1/1/2/4 $23.60 #17

1845 ANNUITY ROLL FOR YEAR
CHIPPEWA, OTTAWA & POTAWATOMI OF MICHIGAN

SILVER CREEK BAND

POKAGON (Chief) 1/1/10/12 $87.72 #1
KEE CHEE WON OH 1/1/5/7 $51.17 #2
SUN AW GO WAW 1/1/6/8 $58.48 #3
WAW GANG CUSH SHICK 1/1/3/5 $36.55 #4
AW GEESH THAY 1/1/8/10 $73.10 #5
CEE THONE 1/1/2/4 $29.24 #6
WEEN GEESE CEE AH 1/1/4/6 $43.86 #7
SAW KEE 1/1/6/8 $58.48 #8
UN UNG GISH 1/1/4/6 $43.86 #9
WEE ZO 0/1/3/4 $29.24 #10
CAW KAY A MAIG 1/1/7/9 $65.79 #11

AW SUTT 1/1/3/5 $36.55 #12
WAY SAW WAY SHUCK 1/1/2/4 $29.24 #13
E DO WAY GEEZHICK 1/1/5/7 $51.17 #14
KAY CAW THAY MO 1/1/2/4 $29.24 #15
SHAW GO SAY MAW 1/1/1/3 $21.93 #16
W USH KISH 1/1/1/3 $21.93 #17
PAY MAW MEE 1/1/6/8 $58.48 #18
PAYMAWMEE, Loui 1/1/0/2 $14.62 #19
MUCCATA KEE QUAY 0/1/2/3 $21.93 #20
MIS SUI A GO QUAY 0/1/3/4 $29.24 #21
MAW GO QUAY 0/1/3/4 $29.24 #22
MAW DIN OH 0/1/2/3 $21.93 #23
AW NAY WEE 1/1/6/8 $58.48 #24
MIN NIS IN O QUAY 0/1/4/5 $36.55 #25

PAW PAW BAND

PEE PEE AW (Chief) 1/1/3/5 $36.55 #1
WAW BIN WAY 1/1/3/5 $36.55 #2
MIS CUN AW 1/1/4/6 $43.86 #3
MIN NAW QUET 1/1/2/4 $29.24 #4
NAY WODGE A GEEZHICK 1/1/2/4 $29.24 #5
WAW BUN O QUAY 1/1/2/4 $29.24 #6
AU GIN EEK 1/1/0/2 $14.62 #7
NAY WAY QUA AW 1/1/1/3 $21.93 #8
CHAW CAW BEE 1/1/1/3 $21.93 #9
E THO IN NAW BEE 1/1/1/3 $21.93 #10
WAUB SIGH 1/1/2/4 $29.24 #11
MAY TAW KEE 1/1/0/2 $14.62 #12

BUSH CREEK BAND

WAW BE MANIDO (Chief) 1/1/4/6 $43.86 #1
SHAY SUCK 1/1/8/10 $73.10 #2
PEE QUAW CUSSEE 1/1/3/5 $36.55 #3
AISH KIB BEE 1/1/1/3 $21.93 #4
A MO NO 1/1/2/4 $29.24 #5
TUSH QUAY AW 0/1/2/3 $21.93 #6

1846 ANNUITY ROLL FOR YEAR
CHIPPEWA, OTTAWA & POTAWATOMI OF MICHIGAN

SILVER CREEK BAND

PO-KA-GON (Chief) 1/1/8/10 $77.80 #1
KEE CHE WAN OH 1/1/4/6 $46.68 #2
SUN AUGH GO AW 1/1/5/7 $54.46 #3
WAW GAW CUS ICK 1/1/4/6 $46.68 #4
AW GES THA 1/1/6/8 $62.24 #5

4

CEE THON 1/1/3/5 $38.90 #6
WEEN GEES CEE AH 1/1/4/6 $46.68 #7
SAW KEE 1/1/6/8 $62.24 #8
UN OO GISH 1/1/5/7 $54.46 #9
WEE ZOO 1/1/3/5 $38.90 #10
KAW KAY A MAY 1/1/3/5 $38.90 #11
AW SUT 1/1/2/4 $31.12 #12
WAY SAW WAY SUT 1/1/2/4 $31.12 #13
SAW GO SAW MAW 1/1/3/5 $38.90 #14
WUSH KISH 1/1/2/4 $31.12 #15
PAY NEES QUAY 0/1/2/3 $23.34 #16
MIS SIN AY GO QUAY 0/1/4/5 $38.90 #17
MAW GO QUAY 0/1/4/5 $38.90 #18
AIN NAY WEE 1/1/6/8 $62.24 #19
MI NIS IN O QUAY 0/1/4/5 $38.90 #20
WE BIN O GE QUAY 1/1/1/3 $23.34 #21
MIS KIN WAY 1/1/3/5 $38.90 #22
TAW GAH 1/1/7/9 $70.02 #23
GET CHE NA GO 1/1/2/4 $31.12 #24
A LEX SEE 1/1/1/3 $23.34 #25
WAMB SIZH 1/1/2/4 $31.12 #26
PAW TESE 1/0/0/1 $7.78 #27
PAY MA MEE 1/1/0/2 $15.56 #28

PAW PAW BAND

A MO NO 1/1/2/4 $31.12 #1
MA GAW QUIS 1/0/0/1 $7.78 #2
WA BIM WAY 0/1/2/3 $23.34 #3
MIN AW QUET 1/1/2/4 $31.12 #4
WA BIM O QUAY 0/1/3/4 $31.12 #5
AU GIN EEK 0/1/2/3 $23.34 #6
NA WAY QUA WAY 0/1/3/4 $31.12 #7
O THO IN AW BAY 2/0/0/2 $15.56 #8
MIS CUN AW 1/1/4/6 $46.68 #9
MA SAW BA TAW 1/1/4/6 $46.68 #10
PEE PEE AW Jun. (Chief) 1/1/4/6 $46.68 #11

BUSH CREEK BAND

WA BI MAN NI DO 1/1/6/8 $62.24 #1
AISH KEE BEE 1/1/4/6 $46.68 #2
PEE QUAW CUSSEE 1/1/3/5 $36.55 #3
AISH KIB BEE 1/1/1/3 $21.93 #4
A MO NO 1/1/2/4 $29.24 #5
TUSH QUAY AW 0/1/2/3 $21.93 #6

5

1847 ANNUITY ROLL FOR YEAR
CHIPPEWA, OTTAWA & POTAWATOMI OF MICHIGAN

SILVER CREEK BAND

PO KA GAN (Chief) 1/1/9/11 $71.50 #1
KU CHU WON AH 1/1/4/6 $39.00 #2
SUM AW GO AW 1/1/5/7 $45.50 #3
WAW GAW CUS SHICK 1/1/6/8 $52.00 #4
AW GUS THAY 1/1/6/8 $52.00 #5
CEE THONE 1/1/3/5 $32.50 #6
WUN GUSE CU AH 1/1/4/6 $39.00 #7
SAW KEE 1/1/6/8 $52.00 #8
UN UG ISH 1/1/3/5 $32.50 #9
WEE ZO 1/1/2/4 $26.00 #10
KAW KAY A MAIG 1/1/2/4 $26.00 #11
AW SUT 1/1/2/4 $26.00 #12
WAY SAW WAW SHUT 1/1/1/3 $19.50 #13
SAW GO SAW MAW 1/1/3/5 $32.50 #14
WIS KISH 1/1/1/3 $19.50 #15
PAY NEESE QUAY 0/1/2/3 $19.50 #16
MIS SIN NAY GO QUAY 0/1/4/5 $32.50 #17
MAW GO QUAY 0/1/4/5 $32.50 #18
AN NAY MU 1/1/6/8 $52.00 #19
MIN NIS IN O QUAY 0/1/4/5 $32.50 #20
WEE BIN O GAQUAY 1/1/2/4 $26.00 #21
MIS KIN WAY 1/1/8/10 $65.00 #22
TAW GAH 1/1/7/9 $58.50 #23
GET CHI NA GO 1/1/0/2 $13.00 #24
A LEX EE 1/1/1/3 $19.50 #25
PAY MAW NU 1/1/2/4 $26.00 #26
TO PASH 1/1/6/8 $52.00 #27
MAY ZO 1/1/4/6 $39.00 #28
MAIS CO 1/0/0/1 $6.50 #29
PAY MAW NUSE, Louis 1/1/0/2 $13.00 #30
E DO WAY GEEZHICK 1/1/4/6 $39.00 #31
KAY CAW DE MO 1/1/3/5 $32.50 #32
PEE MAY O COUT 1/1/0/2 #33

PAW PAW BAND

A MO NO 1/1/2/4 $26.00 #1
MIN AW QUOT 1/1/3/5 $32.50 #2
WAW BIM O QUAY 0/1/3/4 $26.00 #3
AN GIN EEK 0/1/1/2 $13.00 #4
NAY WAY QUAY WA 0/1/2/3 $19.50 #5
O THO IN AW BAY 1/1/1/3 $19.50 #6
MIS CUN AW 1/1/4/6 $39.00 #7
MAW SOB O TAW 1/1/4/6 $39.00 #8
PEE PEE AW Jun. (Chief) 1/1/5/7 $45.50 #9

6

MIS SIGH QUAW GO 1/0/0/1 $6.50 #10

BUSH CREEK BAND

WA BE MAIN NI DO (Chief) 1/1/4/6 $39.00 #1
AISH KE BEE 1/0/0/1 $6.50 #2
NAW WAY QUAY 0/1/1/2 $13.00 #3
WAUB SIGH 1/1/2/4 $26.00 #4
QUO THA QUAY 1/1/1/3 $19.50 #5
NAUGHT TO WAY WISH 1/1/10/12 $78.00 #6

1848 ANNUITY ROLL FOR YEAR
CHIPPEWA, OTTAWA & POTAWATOMI OF MICHIGAN

SILVER CREEK BAND

PO KA GAN (Chief) 1/1/13/15 $86.25 #1
KEE CHE WON OH 1/1/5/7 $40.25 #2
SIN E GO AW 1/1/5/7 $40.25 #3
WAW GAN COO SHICK 1/1/6/8 $46.00 #4
AN GUS THAY 1/1/6/8 $46.00 #5
CEE THONE 1/1/4/6 $34.50 #6
WEEN GEESE SEE AH 1/1/3/5 $28.75 #7
SAW GEE 1/1/5/7 $40.25 #8
UN UG ISH 1/1/3/5 $28.75 #9
KAW KAY A MAIG 1/1/2/4 $23.00 #10
AW SUT 1/1/2/4 $23.00 #11
WAY SAW WAW SHUT 1/1/2/4 $23.00 #12
WIS KISH 1/1/2/4 $23.00 #13
PAY NEE SE QUA 1/1/2/4 $23.00 #14
MIS SIN NAY GO QUA 1/1/2/4 $23.00 #15
MAW GO QUA 0/1/2/3 $17.25 #16
AIN A WEE 1/1/5/7 $40.25 #17
MIN NIS IN O QUA 0/1/4/5 $28.75 #18
MIS KIN WAY 1/1/8/10 $57.50 #19
TAW GAH 1/1/5/7 $40.25 #20
MUSH SHAY A WAY 1/1/1/3 $17.25 #21
GET CHE NA GO 1/1/0/2 $11.50 #22
A LIX EE 1/1/1/3 $17.25 #23
TO PASH 1/1/5/7 $40.25 #24
MAIS COO 1/0/0/1 $5.75 #25
PAY MAW NEESE, Louis 1/1/0/2 $11.50 #26
E DO WAY GEEZHICK 1/1/4/6 $34.50 #27
KAY CAW DE MO 1/1/3/5 $28.75 #28
CHE NE WAY 0/1/2/3 $17.25 #29
O CUM AH WIN 1/1/3/5 $28.75 #30
WAW BIN O QUA 0/1/0/1 $5.75 #31
MAMI GWEE 1/1/2/4 $23.00 #32
O NANG GO 1/1/4/6 $34.50 #33

7

PEE ASH WAY 1/1/6/8 $46.00 #34

PAW PAW BAND

PEE PEE AW (Chief) 1/1/6/8 $46.00 #1
AH DE A NO 1/1/1/3 $17.25 #2
MIS COM AW 1/1/6/8 $46.00 #3
NAY WAY GE GEEZHICK 1/0/0/1 $5.75 #4
MAY MO NEE 1/1/3/5 $28.75 #5
WAS SAW TOO 1/1/6/8 $46.00 #6
WAUB SIGH 1/1/3/5 $28.75 #7
AU TE NAW BAY 1/1/2/4 $23.00 #8
KAW WAW BEN ACE 1/0/0/1 $5.75 #9
CAW GO MAW 1/1/0/2 $11.50 #10
TE QUON 1/0/0/1 $5.75 #11
AEISH KE BEESE 1/0/0/1 $5.75 #12
NAW OH QUA AH 0/1/1/2 $11.50 #13
CHAW MEE 1/1/1/3 $17.25 #14

BUSH CREEK BAND

WAUB BE MAN IDO (Chief) 1/1/5/7 $40.25 #1
KEE ZHICK 1/1/1/3 $17.25 #2
COM NA DA AH 1/1/5/7 $40.25 #3
AISH KEE BEE 1/1/0/2 $11.50 #4
QUO THO QUA 1/1/2/4 $23.00 #5
PEE GWACK CO ZEE 1/1/4/6 $34.50 #6
MEE ZAW 1/1/2/4 $23.00 #7
TUSH QUA GEE ZHICK O QUA 1/1/5/7 $40.25 #8
WEE ZO (2d) 1/1/2/4 $23.00 #9

1849 ANNUITY ROLL FOR YEAR
CHIPPEWA, OTTAWA & POTAWATOMI OF MICHIGAN

SILVER CREEK BAND

POKAGON (Chief) 1/1/11/13 $79.30 #1
KE CHE WAW NO 1/1/5/7 $42.70 #2
SIN E GO WAW 1/1/5/7 $42.70 #3
WAW GAW CO SHICK 1/1/5/7 $42.70 #4
AW GEES THAY 1/1/6/8 $48.80 #5
CE THONG 1/1/3/5 $30.50 #6
WEN GEES SE AH 1/1/4/6 $36.60 #7
SAW GEE 1/1/5/7 $42.70 #8
UN UG ISH 1/0/2/3 $18.30 #9
KAW KAY O MEIG 1/1/2/4 $24.40 #10
AWE SUT 1/1/2/4 $24.40 #11
WAY SAW WAW SHUT 1/1/2/4 $24.40 #12
WISH KISH 1/1/3/5 $30.50 #13

SIN NE SE QUAY 1/1/2/4 $24.40 #14
MIS SIN WAY GO QUAY 1/1/1/3 $18.30 #15
MAW GO QUAY 0/1/2/3 $18.30 #16
AIN E WEE 1/1/5/7 $42.70 #17
MIN NIS IN O QUAY 0/1/3/4 $24.40 #18
MISH KIN WAY 1/2/8/11 $67.10 #19
TAW GAW 1/1/5/7 $42.70 #20
MUSH SHAY A WAY 1/1/2/4 $24.40 #21
GE CHE NAY GO 1/1/0/2 $12.20 #22
COOK SHAY 1/0/3/4 $24.40 #23
TO PASH 1/1/5/7 $42.40 #24
MAISH COO 1/0/0/1 $6.10 #25
CHE NE WAY 0/1/2/3 $18.30 #26
WAW BIN NO QUAY 0/0/2/2 $12.20 #27
MAINE QUEESE 1/1/3/5 $30.50 #28
WAUB SEIGH 1/1/2/4 $24.40 #29
CO WAY ZEE 1/0/0/1 $6.10 #30
E DO WAY GE ZHICK 1/1/4/6 $36.60 #31
KAY KAH DE MO 1/1/3/5 $30.50 #32
O CUM AW WIN 1/1/3/5 $30.50 #33
O NANG GO 1/1/4/6 $36.60 #34
PEE AISH WAY 1/1/6/8 $48.80 #35
PAY MAW NEESE 1/1/3/5 $30.50 #36

PAW PAW BAND

PEE PE AWE (Chief) 2/1/3/6 $36.60 #1
AW DE O NO 1/1/1/3 $18.30 #2
MIS CUM AWE 1/2/4/7 $42.70 #3
NAY WAY GEZHICK 1/1/0/2 $12.20 #4
MAY MO ME 0/1/1/2 $12.20 #5
AN TE NAW BAY 1/1/2/4 $32.40 #6
CAW O GO MAW 1/1/0/2 $12.20 #7
TE QUON 1/0/0/1 $6.10 #8
NAW O QUAY AH 0/1/1/2 $12.20 #9
CAW KEE 1/1/0/2 $12.20 #10

BUSH CREEK BAND

WAUB BE MAIN I DO (Chief) 1/1/5/7 $42.70 #1
CAW ME NO TAY AW 3/2/4/9 $54.90 #2
AISH KE BEE 1/2/1/4 $24.40 #3
QUO THO QUAY 1/1/3/5 $30.50 #4
PE GWACK CO ZEE 1/1/4/6 $36.60 #5
TUSH QUAY GE ZHICK O QUAY 1/1/5/7 $42.70 #6
WEE ZO (2d) 1/1/2/4 $24.40 #7

9

1850 ANNUITY ROLL FOR YEAR
CHIPPEWA, OTTAWA & POTAWATOMI OF MICHIGAN

SILVER CREEK BAND

PO KAY GON (Chief) 1/1/7/9 $65.52 #1
SIN GO WAW (2nd Chief) 1/1/4/6 $43.68 #2
WAW GAW CO SHING 1/1/6/8 $58.24 #3
SE THONE 1/1/4/6 $43.68 #4
QUAY CUSH 0/1/2/3 $21.84 #5
WE ZONE 1/1/3/5 $36.40 #6
SE TOW NACE 1/0/0/1 $7.28 #7
CHE NAY GAW 1/1/1/3 $21.84 #8
CAW CAY O MEIG 1/1/2/4 $29.12 #9
CAW CAW KE 1/1/1/3 $21.84 #10
O SKIN NAW WAY 1/1/5/7 $50.96 #11
WAY GAW WAW SHING 1/1/2/4 $29.12 #12
MAY ME GWEE 1/1/1/3 $21.84 #13
O SAW GEE 1/1/5/7 $50.96 #14
WISH KISH'S Family 1/1/3/5 $36.40 #15
MAISH COO 1/0/0/1 $7.28 #16
CHE NE WAY 0/2/1/3 $21.84 #17
O NAW GISH 1/0/0/1 $7.28 #18
WAW SAY CUM O QUAY 0/2/5/7 $50.96 #19
TAW GAW 0/2/5/7 $50.96 #20
KE CHE WAW NO 1/1/1/3 $21.84 #21
AW SUG 1/1/2/4 $29.12 #22
ME NIS SIN O QUAY 1/1/2/4 $29.12 #23
SHAW GO SE MAW 1/1/0/2 $14.56 #24
AIN NE WE 1/1/5/7 $50.96 #25
PE WAW QUAY NUM 0/2/5/7 $50.96 #26
WACK SE QUAY 0/1/0/1 $7.28 #27
MAW CO PE QUAY 0/1/0/1 $7.28 #28
SIN NE SE QUAY 1/1/2/4 $29.12 #29
WEEN GE SE AW 1/1/3/5 $36.40 #30
ME SHAY WIS 1/1/1/3 $21.84 #31
A CAW TAW MO 1/1/2/4 $29.12 #32
CAW CAW SHAY 1/1/3/5 $36.40 #33

PAW PAW BAND

PE PE AWE (Chief) 1/1/4/6 $43.68 #1
MAY MO NEE 1/0/2/3 $21.84 #2
NAY WAW CHE GE ZHICK 1/1/1/3 $21.84 #3
TE QUON 1/0/0/1 $7.28 #4
CAW O GO MOW 1/0/1/2 $14.56 #5
E TAW E NAW BAY 1/1/2/4 $29.12 #6
CAW KE 1/1/0/2 $14.56 #7
WAW BAW NO QUAY 0/1/2/3 $21.84 #8
PAY MO SAY QUAY 0/1/1/2 $14.56 #9

10

NAW NE ME NUCK SKUNG 1/1/2/4 $29.12 #10
AW TE YEA NO 1/0/1/2 $14.56 #11

BRUSH CREEK BAND

WAW BE MAN I DO (Chief) 1/1/5/7 $50.96 #1
CAW ME NAY TAY AH 1/1/7/9 $65.52 #2
PE QUAW CO ZEE 1/1/4/6 $43.68 #3
QUO THAY QUAY 0/1/4/5 $36.40 #4
NAW O QUAY YAW 0/1/1/2 $14.56 #5
KAY BAISH KUNG 1/0/0/1 $7.28 #6
TUSH QUAY GE ZHICK O QUAY 1/1/6/8 $58.24 #7
AISH KE BE 1/1/3/5 $36.40 #8

1851 ANNUITY ROLL FOR YEAR
CHIPPEWA, OTTAWA & POTAWATOMI OF MICHIGAN

BRUSH CREEK BAND

WAW BE MAN I DO (Chief) 1/1/2/4 $27.72 #1
WILLIAM 1/1/0/2 $13.86 #2
SO ZAY 1/0/0/1 $6.93 #3
CAW ME NO TAY AH 1/0/0/1 $6.93 #4
WAY ME QUAW SAY 1/0/0/1 $6.93 #5
MAW CHE WE TAW 1/1/4/6 $41.58 #6
NAY TAW WAY WISH 1/1/1/3 $20.79 #7
MAN I DO QUE WE ZANCE 1/1/5/7 $43.51 #8
O WISH TE AW 1/0/0/1 $6.93 #9
JOHN 1/1/3/5 $34.65 #10
PE QUAW CO SAY 1/1/3/5 $34.65 #11
PAY SHAW BAW NO QUAY 0/1/0/1 $6.93 #12
NAW NE ME NUCK SKUNG 1/1/2/4 $27.72 #13
MICH SE NAW BAY 1/0/0/1 $6.93 #14
WE ZO 1/1/3/5 $34.65 #15
CAW KE 1/0/0/1 $6.93 #16
TE QUON 1/0/0/1 $6.93 #17

PAW PAW BAND

PE PE AWE (Chief) 1/1/4/6 $41.58 #1
MAM O NEE 0/1/0/1 $6.93 #2
SHAW WAW MAY BE NAY 1/1/0/2 $13.86 #3
AW TE YEA NO 1/0/1/2 $13.86 #4
NAW WAY QUAY YAW 0/1/1/2 $13.86 #5
E TAW WE NAW BAY 1/0/0/1 $6.93 #6
O JIB WAY 1/1/1/3 $20.79 #7
AISH KE BE 1/1/1/3 $20.79 #8
KE SO 0/1/1/2 $13.86 #9
O ME NE SE NO GO QUAY 0/1/0/1 $6.93 #10

PAY MO SAY QUAY 0/1/1/2 #13.86 #11
NAW WAW CHE GE ZHICK 1/1/1/3 $20.79 #12
O NAY GISH 1/0/0/1 $6.93 #13
WAUB SIGH 1/1/3/5 $34.65 #14
ME SHE QUAN GAY 1/1/0/2 $13.86 #15
KAY BAISH KUNG 1/0/0/1 $6.93 #16
WAW BAW NO QUAY 1/1/0/2 $13.86 #17

RUSH LAKE BAND

SIN GO WAW (Chief) 1/1/4/6 $41.58 #1
SE THONE 1/1/4/6 $41.58 #2
SE THONE (2) 1/0/0/1 $6.93 #3
CHE NAY GO 1/1/1/3 $20.79 #4
MAW CAW PE QUAY 0/1/0/1 $6.93 #5
O PAW MO QUAY 0/1/0/1 $6.93 #6
QUE GO NO 1/1/3/5 $34.65 #7
QUAY CUSH 0/1/1/2 $13.86 #8
O SKIN NAW WAY 1/1/5/7 $48.51 #9
CAW GE GAY MEIG 1/0/1/2 $13.86 #10
PAISH CAW ME GO 0/1/1/2 $13.86 #11
CAW CAW KE 1/1/1/3 $20.79 #12
KE SHE GO QUAY 0/1/0/1 $6.93 #13
NAW WE TAY AW MO QUAY 0/1/2/3 $20.79 #14
CAW O GO MO 1/0/0/1 $6.93 #15
WAY ZAW O SHING 1/1/1/3 $20.79 #16
SO ZAY 1/1/3/5 $34.65 #17
O SAW GEE 1/0/0/1 $6.93 #18
MEM GWAY 1/1/1/3 $20.79 #19
WAW CAW CO SHING 1/1/3/5 #20
WAN KE WAY 1/0/0/1 $6.93 #21
WAIN GE SE YAW 1/1/1/3 $20.79 #22
O GE MAW QUAY 0/1/1/2 $13.86 #23
TAW GAW 0/1/3/4 $27.72 #24
NE BAW WE 0/1/2/3 $20.79 #25
ME SHAY WIS 1/1/1/3 #26
CHE NE WAY 0/1/1/2 $13.86 #27

SILVER CREEK BAND

PO KAY GON (Chief) 1/1/6/8 $55.44 #1
JAMES 1/0/0/1 $6.93 #2
MAW CAW SHAW 1/0/0/1 $6.93 #3
MAW NE AWN 0/1/0/1 $6.93 #4
MOOSE 1/1/0/2 $13.86 #5
KE CHE WAW NO 1/1/1/3 $20.79 #6
SHAW GO SE MAW 1/0/0/1 $6.93 #7
AW SUG 1/1/2/4 $27.72 #8
PE WAW QUAY NUM 0/1/4/5 $34.65 #9
NE CO NAY 0/1/0/1 $6.93 #10

12

PAY KE QUAY 0/1/0/1 $6.93 #11
WALK SHE QUAY 0/1/0/1 $6.93 #12
AIN NE WE 0/1/4/5 $34.65 #13
JOHN 1/0/0/1 $6.93 #14
MAWNEE 0/1/0/1 $6.93 #15
SIN NE SE QUAY 1/1/1/3 $20.79 #16
NANCY 0/1/0/1 $6.93 #17
WAW SAY CAW MO QUAY 0/1/5/6 $41.58 #18
WAW ZHO 0/1/0/1 $6.93 #19
E DO WE GE ZHICK 1/1/4/6 $41.58 #20
MAY TWAISH MAW 1/0/0/1 $6.93 #21
QUAY TAW 0/1/0/1 $6.93 #22
CAW CAW SHAY 1/1/3/5 $34.65 #23
VICTORIA 0/1/0/1 $6.93 #24
LAWRENCE 1/0/0/1 $6.93 #25

1852 ANNUITY ROLL FOR YEAR
CHIPPEWA, OTTAWA & POTAWATOMI OF MICHIGAN

PAW PAW BAND

PE PE AWE (Chief) 1/1/5/7 $51.87 #1
MAM O NEE 0/1/0/1 $7.41 #2
SHAW WAW NAY BE NAY SE 1/1/1/3 $22.23 #3
AW TE YEA NO 1/0/0/1 $7.41 #4
NAW WAY QUAY YAW 0/1/1/2 $14.82 #5
E TAW WE NAW BAY 1/0/0/1 $7.41 #6
O JIB WAY 1/1/2/4 $29.64 #7
PAY MO SAY QUAY 0/1/1/2 $14.82 #8
NAW WAW CHE GE ZHICK, Wid. & Niece 0/1/1/2 $14.82 #9
O NAY GISH 1/1/1/3 $22.23 #10
WAUB SIGH 1/1/3/5 $37.05 #11
ME SHE QUAWN GAY 1/1/0/2 #14.82 #12
KAY BAISH KUNG 1/0/0/1 $7.41 #13
WAW BAW NO QUAY 0/1/1/2 $14.82 #14

RUSH LAKE BAND

SIN GO WAW (Chief) 1/1/4/6 $44.46 #1
SE THONE 1/1/4/6 $44.46 #2
SE THONE 2nd 1/0/0/1 $7.41 #3
CHE NAY GO 1/1/2/4 $29.64 #4
MAW CAW PE QUAY 0/1/0/1 $7.41 #5
O PAW MO QUAY 0/1/0/1 $7.41 #6
QUE GO NO 1/1/2/4 $29.64 #7
QUAY CUSH 0/1/1/2 $14.82 #8
O SKIN NAW WAY 1/0/4/5 $37.05 #9
CAW GE GAY MEIG 1/0/1/2 $14.82 #10
PAISH CAW ME GO 0/1/1/2 $14.82 #11

CAW CAW KE 1/1/1/3 $22.23 #12
KE SHE GO QUAY 0/1/0/1 $7.41 #13
CAW O GO MO 1/0/1/2 $14.82 #14
WAY ZAW O SHING 1/1/2/4 $29.64 #15
SO ZAY 1/0/4/5 $37.05 #16
MAY MAW GWEE 1/1/2/4 $29.64 #17
WAW CAW CO SHING, Wid. & Chil. 0/1/4/5 $37.05 #18
O WAN KE WAY 1/0/0/1 $7.41 #19
WAIN GE SE YAW 1/1/2/4 $29.64 #20
O GE MAW QUAY 0/1/1/2 $14.82 #21
O TAW GAW 0/1/3/4 $29.64 #22
NE BAW WE 0/1/2/3 $22.23 #23
CHE NE WAY 0/1/0/1 $7.41 #24

BRUSH CREEK BAND

WAW BE MAN I DO (Chief) 0/1/3/4 $29.64 #1
WILLIAM 1/1/0/2 $14.82 #2
CAW ME NO TAY AH 1/0/0/1 $7.41 #3
WAY ME QUAW SAY 1/0/0/1 $7.41 #4
MAW CHE WE TAW 1/1/4/6 $44.46 #5
NAW TAW WAY WISH 1/1/1/3 $22.23 #6
MAN E DO QUE WE SANSE 1/1/5/7 $51.87 #7
O WISH TE AWE 1/0/0/1 $7.41 #8
JOHN 1/1/3/5 $37.05 #9
PE QUAW CO SAY 1/1/3/5 $37.05 #10
NAW NE ME NUCK SKUNG 1/1/3/5 $37.05 #11
MICK SE NAW BAY 1/0/0/1 $7.41 #12
WE ZO 1/1/3/5 $37.05 #13
CAW KE 1/0/0/1 $7.41 #14
TE QUON 1/0/0/1 $7.41 #15
AISH KE BE 1/1/1/3 $22.23 #16

SILVER CREEK BAND

PO KAY GON (Chief) 1/1/8/10 $74.10 #1
MOOSE 1/1/2/4 $29.64 #2
ME SHAY WIS 1/1/1/3 $22.23 #3
ME NE SE NO GO QUAY 0/1/0/1 $7.41 #4
KE CHE WAW NO 1/1/1/3 $22.23 #5
SHAW GO SE MAW 1/0/0/1 $7.41 #6
AU SUG 1/1/2/4 $29.64 #7
PE WAW QUAY NUM 0/1/5/6 $44.46 #8
PAY KE QUAY 0/1/0/1 $7.41 #9
WALK SHE QUAY 0/1/0/1 $7.41 #10
AIN NE WE 0/1/5/6 $44.46 #11
SIN NE SE QUAY 0/1/2/3 $22.23 #12
WAW SAY CAW NO QUAY 0/1/4/5 $37.05 #13
WAW ZHO 0/1/0/1 $7.41 #14
QUAY TAW 0/1/0/1 $7.41 #15

14

CAW CAW SHAY 1/0/3/4 $29.64 #16

1853 ANNUITY ROLL FOR YEAR
CHIPPEWA, OTTAWA & POTAWATOMI OF MICHIGAN

PAW PAW BAND

PEPE AWE (Chief) 1/2/5/8 $57.92 #1
MAW MO ME 0/1/0/1 $7.24 #2
NAW WAY QUAY YAW 0/1/1/2 $14.48 #3
OJIB WAY 1/1/3/5 $36.20 #4
MO SAY QUAY 0/1/1/2 $14.48 #5
ONAY GISH 1/1/1/3 $21.72 #6
WAUB SIGH 1/1/3/5 $36.20 #7
KAY BAISH KUNG 1/0/0/1 $7.24 #8
MAW NEE 1/1/0/2 $14.48 #9
CAWTAW GEZHICK 1/1/2/4 $28.96 #10
PE AUE 1/1/3/5 $36.20 #11
KE ZO QUAY 0/1/1/2 #14.48 #12
SQUAW CHAW 1/1/0/2 $14.48 #13
PE NAY SE QUAY 1/1/0/2 $14.48 #14

RUSH LAKE BAND

SIN GO WAW (Chief) 1/1/3/5 $36.20 #1
SE THONE 1st 1/1/4/6 $43.44 #2
SE THONE 2nd 1/1/0/2 $14.48 #3
CHE NAY GO 1/1/3/5 $36.20 #4
OPAW MO QUAY 0/1/0/1 $7.24 #5
QUE GO NO 1/1/3/5 $36.20 #6
QUAY CUSH QUAY 0/1/0/1 $7.24 #7
OSKE NAW WAY 1/1/4/6 $43.44 #8
CAW GE GAY MEIG 1/0/1/2 $14.48 #9
PAISH CAW ME GO 0/1/1/2 $14.48 #10
CAW CAW KEE'S, Wife & Child 0/1/1/2 $14.48 #11
KE SHE GO QUAY 0/1/0/1 $7.24 #12
CAW O GO MO 1/1/2/4 $28.96 #13
WAY ZAY O SHING 1/1/1/3 $21.72 #14
SO ZAY & Bros. 3/0/0/3 $21.72 #15
MAY MAW GWEE 1/1/2/4 $28.96 #16
WAIN GE SE GAW 1/1/2/4 $28.96 #17
OGE MAW QUAY 0/1/1/2 $14.48 #18
AIN NE MICK E WAY BE 1/0/0/1 $7.24 #19
OTAW ZHE WAW 0/1/4/5 $36.20 #20
CHE PE CHE WAY GO 1/1/2/4 $28.96 #21
NAW TAY MO QUAY 0/1/1/2 $14.48 #22

15

BRUSH CREEK BAND

WAW BE MAW NE DO (Chief) 0/1/3/4 $28.96 #1
WILLIAM 1/1/0/2 $14.48 #2
CAW ME NO TAY AW 1/0/0/1 $7.24 #3
MAW CHE WE TAW 1/1/4/6 $43.44 #4
MAW NE DO QUE WE SAUSE 1/1/5/7 $50.68 #5
O WISH TE AWE 1/0/0/1 #7.24 #6
JOHN 1/1/4/6 $43.44 #7
PE QUAW CO SAY 1/1/3/5 $36.20 #8
NAW NE ME NUCK SKING 1/1/3/5 $36.20 #9
WE ZO 1/1/4/6 $43.44 #10
CAW KEE 1/0/0/1 $7.24 #11
PE QUON 1/1/1/3 $21.72 #12
AISH KE BE 1/1/0/2 $14.48 #13
TUSH QUAY GE ZHE GO QUAY 0/1/1/2 $14.48 #14
AW TE YEA NO 1/0/0/1 $7.24 #15

SILVER CREEK BAND

POKAYGON, Peter (Chief) 1/1/6/8 $57.92 #1
MOOSE 1/1/2/4 $28.96 #2
ME NIS SE NO QUAY 0/1/0/1 $7.24 #3
KECHE WAW NO 1/0/0/1 $7.24 #4
SHAW GO SE MAW 1/0/1/2 $14.24 #5
AU SUG 1/1/2/4 $28.96 #6
PE WAW QUAY NUM QUAY 0/1/5/6 $43.44 #7
PAY KE QUAY 0/1/0/1 $7.24 #8
WALK SHE QUAY 0/1/0/1 $7.24 #9
AIN NE WE QUAY 0/1/5/6 $43.44 #10
SIN NE SE QUAY 0/1/2/3 $21.72 #11
QUAY TAW 0/1/0/1 $7.24 #12
CAW CAW SHAY 1/0/3/4 $28.96 #13
OTAW GAW 0/1/2/3 $21.72 #14
NE BAW WE QUAY 0/1/2/3 $21.72 #15
CHE NE WAY 0/1/0/1 $7.24 #16
JAMES 1/1/0/2 $14.48 #17
MAW KOONSE 1/0/0/1 $7.24 #18
MARY ANN 0/1/0/1 $7.41 #19

1854 ANNUITY ROLL FOR YEAR
CHIPPEWA, OTTAWA & POTAWATOMI OF MICHIGAN

PAW PAW BAND

PE PE AWE (Chief) 1/2/3/6 $40.32 #1
MAW MO ME 0/1/0/1 $6.72 #2
NAW WAY QUAY YAW 0/1/1/2 $13.44 #3
O JIB WAY 1/1/3/5 $33.60 #4

16

```
MO SAY QUAY 0/1/1/2 $13.44 #5
O NAY GISH 1/1/1/3 $20.16 #6
WAUB SIGH 1/1/4/6 $40.32 #7
KAY BAISH KUNG 1/0/0/1 $6.72 #8
CAW TAW GE ZHICK 1/1/2/4 $26.88 #9
PE AUE 1/1/2/4 $26.88 #10
KY ZO QUAY 0/1/2/3 #20.16 #11
SQUAW CHAW 1/1/0/2 $13.44 #12
KEY WAY SE QUAY 1/1/1/3 $20.16 #13
AW TE AY NAW 1/1/2/4 $26.88 #14
MIS KEY YAW 1/0/0/1 $6.72 #15
ME SE NO GO QUAY 0/1/1/2 $13.44 #16
ME SO QUAW GAY 1/0/0/1 $6.72 #17
```

RUSH LAKE BAND

```
SIN GO WAW (Chief) 1/1/3/5 $33.60 #1
SE THONE 1st 1/1/3/5 $33.60 #2
SE THONE 2nd 1/1/0/2 $13.44 #3
CHE NAY GO 1/1/3/5 $33.60 #4
O PAW MO QUAY 0/1/0/1 $6.72 #5
QUE GO NO 1/1/3/5 $33.60 #6
QUAY CUSH QUAY 0/1/0/1 $6.72 #7
O SKE NAW WAY 1/1/5/7 $47.04 #8
CAW GE GAY MEIG 1/0/1/2 $13.44 #9
PAISH CAW ME GO 0/1/1/2 $13.44 #10
CAW CAW CUS, Wife 0/1/1/2 $13.44 #11
KEY GHE GO QUAY 0/1/0/1 $6.72 #12
CAW O GO MO 1/1/2/4 $26.88 #13
WAY ZAW O SHING 1/1/2/4 $26.88 #14
MAY MAW GUE 1/1/1/3 $20.16 #15
WAIN GE SE YAM 1/1/3/5 $33.60 #16
O GE MAW QUAY 0/1/1/2 $13.44 #17
A NE ME CHE WAY BE 1/0/0/1 $6.72 #18
O TAW ZHE WAW 0/1/5/6 $40.32 #19
CHE PE CHE WAY ZO 1/1/2/4 $26.88 #20
NAW TAY MO QUAY 0/1/1/2 $13.44 #21
```

BRUSH CREEK BAND

```
WAW BE MAN I DO (Chief) 0/1/1/2 $13.44 #1
WILLIAM 1/1/0/2 $13.44 #2
CAW NE NO TAY AW 1/0/0/1 $6.72 #3
MAW CHE WE TAW 1/1/5/7 $47.04 #4
MAW NE TO QUE WE SAUSE 1/1/5/7 $47.04 #5
O WISH TE AWE 1/1/0/2 #13.44 #6
PE QUAW CO SAY 1/1/3/5 $33.60 #7
NAW NE ME NAISH KUNG 1/1/3/5 $33.60 #8
WE ZO 1/1/5/7 $47.04 #9
CAW KEE 0/1/0/1 $6.72 #10
```

PE QUON 1/1/1/3 $20.16 #11
AISH KEY BE 1/1/1/3 $20.16 #12
TUSH QUAY GE ZHE E GO QUAY 0/1/1/2 $13.44 #13
AW TE YEA NO 1/0/0/1 $6.72 #14
NAW TAW WAY WOSH 1/1/0/2 $13.44 #15
TAW CAW WAW GAY 1/1/1/3 $20.16 #16
ME ME GWON SAY 1/0/0/1 $6.72 #17
JOHN & AW TAY QUAY 1/1/4/6 $40.32 #18

SILVER CREEK BAND

KEY CHE WAY NO (Chief) 1/0/0/1 $6.72 #1
POKAYGON, Peter Family 0/1/6/7 $47.04 #2
MOOSE 1/1/2/4 $26.88 #3
ME NE SE NO QUAY 0/1/0/1 $6.72 #4
SAW GAW SE MAW 1/1/1/3 $20.16 #5
AU SUG 1/1/2/4 $26.88 #6
PE WAW GWAW NO QUAY 0/1/5/6 $40.32 #7
PAY KEY QUAY 0/1/0/1 $6.72 #8
WALK SHE QUAY 0/1/0/1 $6.72 #9
AIN NE WE QUAY 0/1/5/6 $40.32 #10
SIN NE SE QUAY 0/1/2/3 $20.16 #11
QUAY TAW 0/1/0/1 $6.72 #12
CAW CAW KEY SHAY 1/0/3/4 $26.88 #13
O TAW GAW 0/1/3/4 $26.88 #14
NE BAW NE QUAY 0/1/2/3 $20.16 #15
CHE NE WAY 0/1/1/2 $13.44 #16
JAMES 1/1/1/3 $20.16 #17
WAW KOONSE 1/0/0/1 $6.72 #18
MARY ANN 0/1/1/2 $13.44 #19

1855 ANNUITY ROLL FOR YEAR
CHIPPEWA, OTTAWA & POTAWATOMI OF MICHIGAN

PAW PAW BAND

PE PE AWE 1/2/5/7 $47.04 #1
MAW MO ME 0/1/2/3 $20.16 #2
NAW WAY QUAY YAW 0/1/2/3 $20.16 #3
O NAY GISH 1/1/1/3 $20.16 #4
WAUB SIGH 1/1/3/5 $33.60 #5
CAW TAW GE ZHICK 1/1/2/4 $26.88 #6
SQUAW CHAW 1/1/1/3 $20.16 #7
KE WAY SE QUAY 0/1/2/3 $20.16 #8
AW TE AY NO 1/1/0/2 $13.44 #9
MIS KE YAW 1/0/0/1 $6.72 #10
ME SO QUAW GAY 1/0/0/1 $6.72 #11
SIN GO WAH 1/1/3/5 $33.60 #12
CE THONE 1st 1/1/3/5 $33.60 #13

CE THONE 2nd 1/1/1/3 $20.16 #14
CHE NAY GO 1/1/3/5 $33.60 #15
O PAW MO QUAY 0/1/0/1 $6.72 #16
QUE GO NO 1/1/4/6 $40.32 #17
QUAY CUSH QUAY 0/1/0/1 $6.72 #18
O SKE NAW WAY 1/1/5/7 $47.04 #19
CAW GE GAY MEG 1/1/0/2 $13.44 #20
PAIS CAW ME GO 0/1/0/1 $6.72 #21
CAW O GO MO 1/0/0/1 $6.72 #22
JACKSON 1/0/1/2 $13.44 #23
WAY ZAW O SHING 1/1/1/3 $20.16 #24
MAY MAW QUE 1/1/0/2 $13.44 #25
WAIN GE SE YAW 1/1/3/5 $33.60 #26
O GE MAW QUA 0/1/1/2 $13.44 #27
A NE CHE WAY BE 1/0/0/1 $6.72 #28
O TAW ZHE WAW 0/1/2/3 $20.16 #29
CHE PE CHE WAY NO 1/1/2/4 $26.88 #30
WAY TE MO QUAY 0/1/1/2 $13.44 #31
WAW BE MAN I TO 0/1/1/2 $13.44 #32
WILLIAM 1/1/0/2 $13.44 #33
CAW NE NO TAY AW 1/0/0/1 $6.72 #34
MAW CHE NE TAW 1/1/4/6 $40.32 #35
MAN I TO QUE NE SAUCE 1/1/5/7 $47.04 #36
O WISH TE AWE 1/0/0/1 #6.72 #37
PE QUAY CO SE 1/1/1/3 $20.16 #38
NAW NE ME NAISH KUNG 1/1/3/5 $33.60 #39
WE ZO 1/1/5/7 $47.04 #40
KAW KEE 1/1/0/2 $13.44 #41
TE QUON 1/1/1/3 $20.16 #42
AISH KE BE 1/1/4/6 $40.32 #43
WAW TAW WAY WISH 1/0/0/1 $6.72 #44
SAY CAW MAW GAY 1/1/1/3 $20.16 #45
MAY ME QUON SAY 1/1/0/2 $13.44 #46
JOHN 1/1/4/6 $40.32 #47
KEY CHE WAY NO (Chief) 1/0/0/1 $6.72 #48
POKAYGON, Peter Family 0/1/6/7 $47.04 #49
AW MORE 1/1/4/6 $40.32 #50
SAW GAW SE MAW 1/1/1/3 $20.16 #51
AU SAG 1/1/2/4 $26.88 #52
PE WAW QUA NUM 0/1/5/6 $40.32 #53
PAY KE QUAY 0/1/0/1 $6.72 #54
WAWK SHE QUAY 0/1/0/1 $6.72 #55
AIN NE WE QUAY 0/1/5/6 $40.32 #56
SIN NE SE QUAY 0/1/2/3 $20.16 #57
QUAY TAW 0/1/0/1 $6.72 #58
KAW KAW KE CHA 1/0/3/4 $26.88 #59
O TAW GAW 0/1/3/4 $26.88 #60
WE BAW WE QUAY 0/1/2/3 $20.16 #61
CHE NE WAY 0/1/1/2 $13.44 #62
JAMES 1/1/1/3 $20.16 #63

19

WAW SAW TO 1/1/2/4 $26.88 #64
BAT TISE 1/1/4/6 $40.32 #65
KE ZHICK 1/1/0/2 $13.44 #66
MAIM GREE, Mary Ann 0/1/1/2 $13.44 #67
NAW O KEE 1/1/1/3 $20.16 #68
SIN NE GO QUAY 0/1/1/2 $13.44 #69
WO ZHO, Mary 0/1/0/1 $6.72 #70
WAW SO 1/1/3/5 $33.60 #71
WE ZO 1/1/0/2 $13.44 #72
WAW KE WAY 1/0/0/1 $6.72 #73

1856 ANNUITY ROLL FOR YEAR
CHIPPEWA, OTTAWA & POTAWATOMI OF MICHIGAN

PAW PAW BAND

PE PE AH (Chief) 1/1/3/5 $35.90 #1
MA MO NE 0/1/1/2 $14.36 #2
NAH WA QUA YAH 0/1/2/3 $21.54 #3
O NA GISH 1/1/1/3 $21.54 #4
WAB SI 1/1/4/6 $43.08 #5
KAH TAH GE ZHICK 1/1/2/4 $28.72 #6
SQUAH CHAH 1/1/1/3 $21.54 #7
AH TE A NO 1/0/0/1 $7.18 #8
MIS KE YAH 1/0/0/1 $7.18 #9
ME SO QUON GA 1/0/0/1 $7.18 #10
AISH KE BE 1/1/2/4 $28.72 #11
PE WA SE QUAY 0/1/1/2 $14.36 #12
WAH SAH TO 1/0/2/3 $21.54 #13
BATTISE 1/1/3/5 $35.90 #14
KE ZHICK 1/1/0/2 $14.36 #15
MARY ANN 0/1/1/2 $14.36 #16
WAH SO 1/1/3/5 $35.90 #17
MO SO 1/0/0/1 $7.18 #18
SIN GO WAH 1/1/3/5 $35.90 #19
SE THONE 1st 1/1/3/5 $35.90 #20
SE THONE 2nd 1/1/1/3 $21.54 #21
CHE NA GO 1/1/2/4 $28.72 #22
QUA GO NO 1/1/4/6 $43.08 #23
QUA CASH QUA 0/1/0/1 $7.18 #24
O SKE NAH WA 1/1/5/7 $50.25 #25
KAH GE GA MY 1/1/0/2 $14.36 #26
MA ME GWAH 1/1/0/2 $14.36 #26
KAH O GO MO 1/0/0/1 $7.18 #27
JACKSON 2/0/0/2 $14.36 #28
WAH SAH O SHICK 1/1/0/2 $14.36 #29
MA ME GWE 1/1/1/3 $21.54 #30
WAIN GE ZE YAH 1/1/3/5 $35.90 #31
O GE MAH QUA 0/1/1/2 $14.36 #32

20

AH NE ME CHE WA BE 1/0/0/1 $7.18 #33
O TAH ZHE WAH 0/1/2/3 $21.54 #34
SHE PE THE WAH NO 1/1/2/4 $28.72 #35
MAH TA MO QUA 0/1/1/2 $14.36 #36
WAH BE MAN I TO 0/1/1/2 $14.36 #37
WILLIAM 1/1/0/2 $14.36 #38
MAH CHE WE TAH 1/1/3/5 $35.90 #39
MAN I TO QUE WE SANCE 1/1/4/6 $43.08 #40
NAH WE NE MAISH KUNG 1/1/3/5 $35.90 #41
WE ZO 1/1/6/8 $57.44 #42
KAH KE 1/1/0/2 $14.36 #43
TE QUON 1/1/1/3 $21.54 #44
NAH TA WA WISH 1/0/0/1 $7.18 #45
TA KAH MON GA 1/1/1/3 $21.54 #46
MIX, John 1/1/4/6 $43.08 #47
KE CHE WA NO 1/0/0/1 $7.18 #48
MO SO, Joseph 1/1/1/3 $21.54 #49
SIN NE GO QUA 0/1/1/2 $14.36 #50
POKAYGON, Peter Family 2/1/6/9 $64.62 #51
AH MORE 1/1/2/4 $28.72 #52
SAH GAH SE MO 1/1/1/3 $21.54 #53
AH SICK 1/1/2/4 $28.72 #54
PE WAH GNO NUM 0/1/5/6 $43.08 #55
PA KE QUA 0/1/0/1 $7.18 #56
WAH KE SE QUA 0/1/0/1 $7.18 #57
AIN NE WE QUA 0/1/4/5 $35.90 #58
SIN NEECE QUA 0/1/2/3 $21.54 #59
QUA TAH 0/1/0/1 $7.18 #61
KAH KAH KE SHA 1/1/2/4 $28.72 #62
O TAH GAH 0/1/1/2 $14.36 #63
NE BAH WE QUA 0/1/3/4 $28.72 #64
NAH O KE 1/1/2/4 $28.72 #65
WAH SHO, Mary 0/1/0/1 $7.18 #66
WE ZO 1/1/0/2 $14.36 #67
WAH KE WA 1/0/0/1 $7.18 #68
JOSETTE 0/1/1/2 $14.36 #69
GEORGE 1/1/0/2 $14.36 #70
O NA GO 1/1/0/2 $14.36 #71

1857 ANNUITY ROLL FOR YEAR
CHIPPEWA, OTTAWA & POTAWATOMI OF MICHIGAN

PO KAY GON BAND

PO KAY GON, Francis (Chief) 1/0/1/2 $13.84 #1
AW QUE NAW, Wid. & Chln. 2/2/4/8 $55.36 #2
PO KAY GON, James 1/0/0/1 $6.92 #3
AW SUCK 1/1/2/4 $27.68 #4
MOOSE 1/1/0/2 $13.84 #5

21

NAY NOS 1/1/1/3 $20.76 #6
RAPP, George 1/1/2/4 $27.68 #7
SAW GO SE MAW 1/1/1/3 $20.76 #8
PE WAW QUO UM 0/1/3/4 $27.68 #9
AUGUSTUS, William 1/0/0/1 $6.92 #10
PAY KEY QUAY 0/1/0/1 $6.92 #11
WALK SE QUAY 0/1/0/1 $6.92 #12
AUGUSTUS, Nich. 1/0/0/1 $6.92 #13
KAW KAW KE SHE 1/0/3/4 $27.68 #14
AIN NE WE QUAY 0/1/3/4 $27.68 #15
O NAY GOO 1/1/0/2 $13.84 #16
SIN NE SE QUAY'S Child 0/0/1/1 $6.92 #17
CUSHWAY, John 1/0/0/1 $6.92 #18
MAW NEE TO PUSH 0/1/0/1 $6.92 #19
KE NO NAW NE QUAY 0/1/2/3 $20.76 #20
MAY MO NE 0/1/0/1 $6.92 #21
AW TE AW NO 1/0/0/1 $6.92 #22
MAW SO 1/0/0/1 $6.92 #23
AW TAW QUAW NUM 0/1/1/2 $13.84 #24

SIN GO WAW BAND

SIN GO WAW (Chief) 1/1/4/6 $41.52 #1
SE THONE 1st 1/1/3/5 $34.60 #2
WILLIAM 1/1/0/2 $13.84 #3
SE THONE 2nd 1/1/1/3 $20.76 #4
NAW O QUAY YAW 0/1/1/2 $13.84 #5
CHE NAY GAW 1/1/2/4 $27.68 #6
TE QUON 1/1/1/3 $20.76 #7
WAW SAW TOE 1/0/1/2 $13.84 #8
O PAW ME SAY 0/1/4/5 $34.60 #9
AISH KEY BE 1/1/1/3 $20.76 #10
NAW TAW WAY WISH 1/0/0/1 $6.92 #11
O TAW GAW 0/1/3/4 $27.68 #12
WAUB SIGH 1/1/4/6 $41.52 #13
NAW O KEY 1/1/1/3 $20.76 #14
NE BAW WE QUAY 0/1/3/4 $27.68 #15
QUAY GO NO 1/1/5/7 $48.44 #16
WAW O GIN 1/1/2/4 $27.68 #17
PAY CAW SAY 2/3/1/6 $41.52 #18
QUAY CUSH QUAY 0/1/0/1 $6.92 #19
O SKE NAW WAY 1/1/5/7 $48.44 #20
WAY ME GWAW SAY 1/1/0/2 $13.84 #21
SO ZETTE 0/1/1/2 $13.84 #22
WE ZO 1/1/0/2 $13.84 #23
KAW O GO MO 1/0/0/1 $6.92 #24
KE ZHICK 1/1/0/2 $13.84 #25
JACKSON & Bro. 2/0/0/2 $13.84 #26
TAY CAW MAW GAY 2/0/1/3 $20.76 #27
WAW SAW O ZHICK 1/1/0/2 $13.84 #28

O NAW GISH 1/1/0/2 $13.84 #29
MAY NEE GWE 1/1/1/3 $20.76 #30
SQUAW JAW, John 1/1/1/3 $20.76 #31
WAW GE ZHE YAW 1/1/4/6 $41.52 #32
A KEN 1/1/1/3 $20.76 #33
CHE NE WAY 0/1/2/3 $20.76 #34
O GE MAW QUAY 0/1/0/1 $6.92 #35
KAW KEE 1/1/0/2 $13.84 #36
MAW CHE WE TAW 1/1/4/6 $41.52 #37
NO NE ME CHE NAY BE 1/0/0/1 $6.92 #38
WEZO MO TAY 1/1/6/8 $55.36 #39
NAW NE ME NUCK SKUCK 1/1/3/5 $34.60 #40
SKE PE SHE WAW NO 1/1/2/4 $27.68 #41
PE QUAW KO SAY 1/1/2/4 $27.68 #42
NAW AW TAY AW MO QUAY 0/2/0/2 $13.84 #43
MAW NE DO QUE WE SANSE 1/1/4/6 $41.52 #44
MAISH KEY AWE 1/0/0/1 $6.92 #45
WAW SO 1/1/2/4 $27.68 #46
NAW KEE 1/1/2/4 $27.68 #47
SIN GO QUAY 0/1/1/2 $13.84 #48
MAW SO, Joseph 1/1/1/3 $20.76 #49
MIX, John 1/1/4/6 $41.52 #50

1858 ANNUITY ROLL FOR YEAR
CHIPPEWA, OTTAWA & POTAWATOMI OF MICHIGAN

POKAYGON BAND

POKAYGON, Francis (Chief) 1/1/1/3 $20.34 #1
AW QUE WE NAW & Children 2/2/4/8 $54.24 #2
POKAYGON, James 1/0/0/1 $6.78 #3
AW SUCK 1/1/2/4 $27.12 #4
MOOSE 1/1/0/2 $13.56 #5
NAY NOS 1/1/1/3 $20.34 #6
RAPP, George 1/1/2/4 $27.12 #7
SAW GO SE MAW 1/1/1/3 $20.34 #8
PE WAW QUO UM 0/1/3/4 $27.12 #9
AUGUSTUS, William 1/0/0/1 $6.78 #10
PAY KEY QUAY 0/1/0/1 $6.78 #11
AUGUSTUS, Nicholas 1/0/0/1 $6.78 #12
KAW KAW KE SHE 1/1/3/5 $33.90 #13
AIN NE WE QUAY 0/1/3/4 $27.12 #14
ONAY GOO 1/1/0/2 $13.56 #15
SIN NE SE QUAY'S Child 0/0/1/1 $6.78 #16
CUSHWAY, John 1/0/2/3 $20.34 #17
TOPOSH, Mary 0/1/0/1 $6.78 #18
KE NO NAW NE QUAY 0/1/2/3 $20.34 #19
MAY MO NE 0/1/0/1 $6.78 #20
AW TE AW NO 1/0/0/1 $6.78 #21

MAW SO 1/0/0/1 $6.78 #22
AW DAW GWAW NUM 0/1/1/2 $13.56 #23

SIN GO WAW BAND

SIN GO WAW (Chief) 1/1/4/6 $40.68 #1
NAW O QUAY YAW 0/1/1/2 $13.56 #2
NAW OKEY 1/1/1/3 $20.34 #3
WAW O GIN 1/1/2/4 $27.12 #4
PAY CAW SAY 2/3/1/6 $40.68 #5
WAY ME GWAW SAY 1/1/0/2 $13.56 #6
NAW KEE 1/1/2/4 $27.12 #7
SE THONE 1st 1/1/1/3 $20.34 #8
WILLIAM 1/1/0/2 $13.56 #9
SE THONE 2nd 1/1/4/6 $40.68 #10
CHE NAY GO 1/1/3/5 $33.90 #11
TE QUON 1/1/2/4 $27.12 #12
WAW SAW TOE 1/0/1/2 $13.56 #13
OPAW ME SAY 0/1/4/5 $33.90 #14
AISH KE BE 1/1/1/3 $20.34 #15
NOT TO NAY WISH 1/0/0/1 $6.78 #16
OTAW GAW 0/1/3/4 $27.12 #17
WAUB SIN 1/1/4/6 $40.68 #18
NE BAW WE QUAY 0/1/3/4 $27.12 #19
QUAY GO NO 1/1/4/6 $40.68 #20
QUAY CUSH QUAY 0/1/0/1 $6.78 #21
OSKE NAW WAY 1/1/4/6 $40.68 #22
SOZETTE 0/1/1/2 $13.56 #23
WE ZO 1/1/0/2 $13.56 #24
KAW O GO MAW 1/0/0/1 $6.78 #25
KE ZHICK 1/1/1/3 $20.34 #26
JACKSON & Bro. 2/0/0/2 $13.56 #27
TAY CAW MAW GAY 2/0/1/3 $20.34 #28
WAW SAW OZHICK 1/1/1/3 $20.34 #29
ONAY GISH 1/1/0/2 $13.56 #30
MAY ME GWE 1/1/1/3 $20.34 #31
SQUAW JAW, John 1/1/2/4 $27.12 #32
WAN GE ZHE YAW 1/1/3/5 $33.90 #33
AKEN 1/1/2/4 $27.12 #34
CHE NE WAY 0/1/2/3 $20.34 #35
OGE MAW QUAY 0/1/0/1 $6.78 #36
KAW KE 1/0/0/1 $6.78 #37
MAW CHE WE TAW 1/1/3/5 $33.90 #38
AW NE ME CHE WAY BE 1/0/0/1 $6.78 #39
WEZO MO TAY 1/1/5/7 $47.46 #40
NAW NE ME NUCK SKUCK 1/1/4/6 $40.68 #41
SHEPE SHE WAW NO 1/1/2/4 $27.12 #42
PE QUAW KO SAY 1/1/1/3 $20.34 #43
NAW AW LAY AW MO QUAY 0/2/0/2 $13.68 #44
MAW NE DO QUE WE SAUSE 1/1/4/6 $40.68 #45

SIN GO QUAY 0/1/1/2 $13.68 #46
MAWSO, Joseph 1/1/2/4 $27.12 #47
MIX, John 1/1/5/7 $47.46 #48
WAW SO 1/1/2/4 $27.12 #49

1859 ANNUITY ROLL FOR YEAR
CHIPPEWA, OTTAWA & POTAWATOMI OF MICHIGAN

PO KAY GON BAND

PO KAY GON, Fr. (Chief) 1/0/0/1 $6.27 #1
AW QUE WE NAW 2/2/4/8 $50.16 #2
PO KAY GON, James 1/0/1/2 $12.54 #3
AW SUCK 1/1/2/4 $25.08 #4
MOOSE 1/1/0/2 $12.54 #5
NAY NOS 0/1/2/3 $18.81 #6
RAPP, Geo. 1/1/2/4 $25.08 #7
SAW GO SE MAW 1/1/2/4 $25.08 #8
PE WAW QUO UM 0/1/3/4 $25.08 #9
AUGUSTUS, Wm. 1/0/0/1 $6.27 #10
PAY KEY QUAY 0/1/0/1 $6.27 #11
AUGUSTUS, Nich. 1/1/1/3 $18.81 #12
KAW KAW KAW SHE 1/0/5/6 $37.62 #13
AIN NE NE QUAY 0/1/2/3 $18.81 #14
O NAY GOO 1/1/0/2 $12.54 #15
KIN NE SE QUAY Child 0/0/1/1 $6.27 #16
CUSHWAY, John 1/0/0/1 $6.27 #17
MAW NE TOPOSH 0/1/0/1 $6.27 #18
KE NO NAW NE QUAY 0/1/3/4 $25.08 #19
MAY MO NEE 0/1/0/1 $6.27 #20
AW TE AW NO 1/0/0/1 $6.27 #21
MAW SO 1/0/0/1 $6.27 #22
AW DAW QWAW NUM 0/1/0/1 $6.27 #23
PAY SHE AW WAY, John P. 1/1/4/6 $37.62 #24
WAUB CHE CHALK 1/0/0/1 $6.27 #25
AT QUAY WEE 0/1/0/1 $6.27 #26
BEE BEECE 0/1/0/1 $6.27 #27
O GE WAW WEE 1/1/4/6 $37.62 #28
KAW NE SAW QUAY 0/1/3/4 $25.08 #29
MAY TWAY SE MAW 1/0/0/1 $6.27 #30

SIN GO WAW BAND

SIN GO WAW (Chief) 1/1/2/4 $25.08 #1
WAW GAW CO WE NAW, Mrs. 0/1/0/1 $6.27 #2
KAW KAW KEE, Mrs. 0/1/0/1 $6.27 #3
NAW O QUAY YAW 0/1/0/1 $6.27 #4
NAW O KEE 1/1/1/3 $18.81 #5
WAW O GIN 1/1/2/4 $25.08 #6

25

PAY CAW SAW 1/3/1/5 $31.35 #7
MAW CO QUAY 0/1/1/2 $12.54 #8
WAY NEE GWAW SAY 1/0/0/1 $6.27 #9
NAW KEE 1/1/1/3 $28.81 #10
SE THONE 1st 1/1/3/5 $31.35 #11
SE THONE 2nd 1/1/1/3 $18.81 #12
WILLIAM 1/1/0/2 $12.54 #13
KEY CHE NAY GO 1/1/3/5 $31.35 #14
TE QUON 1/1/2/4 $25.08 #15
CHE CAW SCAW AW MO QUAY 0/1/3/4 $25.08 #16
WAW SAW TOO 0/1/0/1 $6.27 #17
JACKSON 1/1/1/3 $18.81 #18
MAW CO TAW 0/0/1/1 $6.27 #19
AISH KE BE 1/1/2/4 $25.08 #20
NAW TAW WAY WISH 1/0/0/1 $6.27 #21
WAUB SIGH 1/1/3/5 $31.35 #22
PARSONS, Mrs. Levi 0/1/4/5 $31.35 #23
QUAY GO NO 1/1/5/7 $43.89 #24
QUAY CUSH QUAY 0/1/0/1 $6.27 #25
O SKE NAW WAY 1/1/5/7 $43.89 #26
SO ZETTE 0/1/1/2 $12.54 #27
WE ZO 1/1/1/3 $18.81 #28
KAW O GO MO 1/0/0/1 $6.27 #29
KE ZHICK 1/1/1/3 $18.81 #30
WAW GAW CO ZHICK 1/0/0/1 $6.27 #31
TAY CAW MAY GAY 1/0/1/2 $12.54 #32
MAW CAW DAY KE ZHICK 1/0/0/1 $6.27 #33
O WAW NAW KE WAW 1/1/1/3 $18.81 #34
O NAY GISH 1/1/0/2 $12.54 #36
MAY ME GWE 1/1/1/3 $18.81 #37
SQUAW GAW, John 1/1/2/4 $25.08 #38
WAIN GO ZHE YAW 1/1/4/6 $37.62 #39
A KEN 1/1/1/3 $18.81 #40
O GE MAW QUAY 0/1/0/1 $6.27 #41
CHE NE WAY 0/1/2/3 $18.81 #42
KAW KEE, Joseph 1/0/0/1 $6.27 #43
MAW CHE WE TAW 1/1/3/5 $31.35 #44
AW NE ME CHE WAY BE 1/0/0/1 $6.27 #45
WE ZO MO TAY 1/1/5/7 $43.89 #46
NAW NE ME NUCK SHUCK 1/1/4/6 $37.62 #47
SHE PE SHE WAW NO 1/1/1/3 $18.81 #48
TO POSH, Mrs. 0/1/0/1 $6.27 #49
PE QUAW CO SAY 1/1/1/3 $18.81 #50
MAW NE DO QUE WE SAUSE 2/1/4/7 $43.89 #51
SIN GO QUAY 0/1/1/2 $12.54 #52
MAW SO, Joseph 1/1/2/4 $25.08 #53
MIX, John 1/1/5/7 $43.89 #54
WAW SO 1/1/3/5 $31.35 #55

CHIPPEWA, OTTAWA & POTAWATOMI OF MICHIGAN

POKAYGON BAND

POKAYGON, Francis (Chief) 1/0/0/1 $6.72 #1
AW QUE WE NAW 2/2/4/8 $53.76 #2
PO KAY GON, James 1/0/1/2 $13.44 #3
AW SUCK 1/1/2/4 $26.88 #4
MOOSE 1/1/0/2 $13.44 #5
NAY NOS 0/1/2/3 $20.16 #6
RAPP, Geo. 1/1/3/5 $33.60 #7
SAW GO SE MAW 1/1/2/4 $26.88 #8
PE WAW QUO UM 0/1/3/4 $26.88 #9
AUGUSTUS, Wm. 1/0/0/1 $6.72 #10
PAY KEY QUAY 0/1/0/1 $6.72 #11
AUGUSTUS, Mrs. Nich. 0/1/1/2 $13.44 #12
KAW KAW KAW SHE 1/0/5/6 $40.32 #13
RAIL, Mrs. Antwoine 0/1/2/3 $20.16 #14
O NAY NAW GOOSE'S Wife 0/1/0/1 $6.72 #15
KIN NE SE QUAY'S Child 0/0/1/1 $6.72 #16
CUSHWAY, John 1/0/0/1 $6.72 #17
MAW NE TO POSH 0/1/0/1 $6.72 #18
TO POSH, Mrs. 0/1/0/1 $6.72 #19
KE NO NAW NE QUAY 0/1/3/4 $26.88 #20
MAW SO 1/0/0/1 $6.72 #21
AW DAW QUO NUM 0/1/0/1 $6.72 #22
SHE PE SHE WAW NO 1/1/1/3 $20.16 #23

SIN GO WAW BAND

SIN GO WAW (Chief) 1/1/1/3 $20.16 #1
WAW GAW KO WE NAW, Mrs. 0/1/0/1 $6.72 #2
KAW KAW KEE, Mrs. 0/1/0/1 $6.72 #3
NAW O QUAY YAW 0/1/0/1 $6.72 #4
NAW O KEE 1/1/0/2 $13.44 #5
WAW O GIN 1/1/3/5 $33.60 #6
PAY CAW SAW 2/3/2/7 $47.04 #7
WAY ME GWAW SAY 1/0/0/1 $6.72 #8
NAW KEE 1/1/3/5 $33.60 #9
SE THONE 1st 1/1/4/6 $40.32 #10
SE THONE 2nd 1/1/2/4 $26.88 #11
WILLIAM 1/1/1/3 $20.16 #12
KE CHE NAY GO 1/1/3/5 $33.60 #13
TE QUON 1/1/2/4 $26.88 #14
CHE CUSH CAW MO QUAY 0/1/3/4 $26.88 #15
WAW SAW TOE 1/0/1/2 $13.44 #16
JACKSON 1/0/0/1 $6.72 #17
AISH KE BE 1/1/2/4 $26.88 #18
O GE MAW WE 1/1/4/6 $40.32 #19

```
NAW TAW WAY WISH 1/0/0/1 $6.72 #20
WAUB SIGH 1/1/3/5 $33.60 #21
PARSONS, Mrs. Levi 0/1/4/5 $33.60 #22
QUAY GO NO 1/1/5/7 $47.04 #23
QUAY CUSH QUAY 0/1/0/1 $6.72 #24
O SKE NAW WAY 1/1/5/7 $47.04 #25
SO ZETTE 0/1/1/2 $13.44 #26
WE ZO 1/1/0/2 $13.44 #27
KAW O GO MO 1/1/0/2 $13.44 #28
KE ZHICK 1/1/0/2 $13.44 #29
WAW GAW KO ZHICK 1/0/0/1 $6.72 #30
TAY CAW MAY GAY 1/1/2/4 $26.88 #31
MAW CAW DAY KE ZHICK 1/0/0/1 $6.72 #32
O WAW NE KE WAY 1/1/1/3 $20.16 #33
O NAY GISH 1/1/0/2 $13.44 #34
MAY ME GWE 1/1/1/3 $20.16 #35
SQUAW GAW, Mrs. John 0/1/2/3 $20.16 #36
WAIN GE ZHE YAW 1/1/4/6 $40.32 #37
A KEN 1/1/2/4 $26.88 #38
O GE MAW QUAY 0/1/0/1 $6.72 #39
CHE NE WAY 0/1/2/3 $20.16 #40
KAW KE, Joseph 1/0/0/1 $6.72 #41
MAW CHE WE TAW 1/1/3/5 $33.60 #42
WE ZO MO TAY 1/1/5/7 $47.04 #43
NAW NE ME NUCK SKUCK 1/1/4/6 $40.32 #44
PE QUAW CO SAY 1/1/1/3 $20.16 #45
MAW NE DO QUE WE SAUSE 1/1/3/5 $33.60 #46
SIN GO QUAY 0/1/1/2 $13.44 #47
MAW SO, Joseph 1/1/3/5 $33.60 #48
MIX, John 1/1/5/7 $47.04 #49
WAW SO 1/1/2/4 $26.88 #50
KAW O GO MO 2nd 1/0/0/1 $6.72 #51
```

1861 ANNUITY ROLL FOR 4TH QTR
POTAWATOMI OF HURON

```
MAGWAWGO Chief 1/0/0/1 $7.84 #1
MACKIE 1/1/3/5 $39.20 #2
DOGAH 0/1/1/2 $15.68 #3
KAY GWAY DAW SUNG 1/1/3/5 $39.20 #4
NAW CHE WAW NO QUAY 0/1/2/3 $23.52 #5
ME ME 1/1/4/6 $47.04 #6
NAY AW CHE 1/0/0/1 $7.84 #7
PAMP TWAY PE 1/1/0/2 $15.68 #8
PAMP TWAY PE, John 1/1/3/5 $39.20 #9
PAMP TWAY PE, Phineas 1/1/3/5 $39.20 #10
PE NAY MO 1/1/0/2 $15.68 #11
KAY BAISH KUNG 1/0/0/1 $7.84 #12
KESES'S Wife & Child 0/1/1/2 $15.68 #13
```

28

EDOWE KE ZHICK 1/1/3/5 $39.20 #14
NO WAY SAY 0/1/0/1 $7.84 #15
KETOSH 1/0/1/2 $15.68 #16
PAY ME TAY QUO UCK 1/1/1/3 $23.52 #17

1861 ANNUITY ROLL FOR YEAR
CHIPPEWA, OTTAWA & POTAWATOMI OF MICHIGAN

PO KAY GON BAND

PO KAY GON, Francis (Chief) 1/0/0/1 $6.75 #1
AW GWE WE NAW 2/2/4/8 $54.00 #2
PO KAY GON, James 1/0/1/2 $13.50 #3
AW SUCK 1/1/2/4 $27.00 #4
MOOSE 1/1/0/2 $13.50 #5
NAY NOS 0/1/2/3 $20.25 #6
RAPP, Geo. 1/1/3/5 $33.75 #7
SAW GO SE MAW 1/1/3/5 $33.75 #8
PE WAW QUO NUM 0/1/3/4 $27.00 #9
AUGUSTUS, Wm. 1/0/0/1 $6.75 #10
AUGUSTUS, Mrs. Nicholas 0/1/1/2 $13.50 #11
KAW KAW KAW SHE 1/0/5/6 $40.50 #12
RAIL, Mrs. Antoine 0/1/2/3 $20.25 #13
KEN NESEQUAY'S Child 0/0/1/1 $6.75 #14
CUSHWAY, John 1/0/0/1 $6.75 #15
TO POSH, Mrs. 0/1/0/1 $6.75 #16
TOPOSH, Mary 0/1/0/1 $6.75 #17
KE NO NAW NE QUAY 0/1/3/4 $27.00 #18
MAW SO 1/0/0/1 $6.75 #19
AW DAW QUO NUM 0/1/0/1 $6.75 #20
SHE PE SHE WAW NO 1/1/1/3 $20.25 #21
SHAW WAW NAY SO 0/0/1/1 $6.75 #22

SIN GO WAW BAND

SIN GO WAW (Chief) 1/1/0/2 $13.50 #1
WAW GAW KO WE NAW, Mrs. 0/1/0/1 $6.75 #2
NAW O QUAY YAW 0/1/0/1 $6.75 #3
NAW O KEE 1/1/0/2 $13.50 #4
WAW O GIN 1/1/3/5 $33.75 #5
PAY CAW SAW 1/3/2/6 $40.50 #6
MICK SE NOC 1/1/2/4 $27.00 #7
NAW KEE 1/1/2/4 $27.00 #8
SE THONE 1st 1/1/3/5 $33.75 #9
SE THONE 2nd 1/1/2/4 $27.00 #10
WILLIAM 1/1/1/3 $20.25 #11
KE CHE NAY GO 1/1/3/5 $33.75 #12
TE QUON 1/1/3/5 $33.75 #13
CHE CUSH CAW MO QUAY 0/1/3/4 $27.00 #14

29

WAW SAW TOE 1/0/1/2 $13.50 #15
JACKSON 1/0/0/1 $6.75 #16
AISH KE BE 1/1/1/3 $20.25 #17
O GE MAW WE 1/1/4/6 $40.50 #18
NAW TAW WAY WISH 1/1/0/1 $6.75 #19
WAUB SIGH 1/1/3/5 $33.75 #20
PARSONS, Mrs. Levi 0/1/6/7 $47.25 #21
QUAY GO NO 1/1/5/7 $47.25 #22
QUAY CUSH QUAY 0/1/0/1 $6.75 #23
O SKE NAW WAY 1/1/5/7 $47.25 #24
SO ZETTE 0/1/1/2 $13.50 #25
WE ZO 1/1/0/2 $13.50 #26
KAW O GO MO 1/0/0/1 $6.75 #27
KE ZHICK 1/1/0/2 $13.50 #28
WAW GAW KO ZHICK 1/0/0/1 $6.75 #29
TAY CAW MAW GAY 1/1/3/5 $33.75 #30
MAW CAW DAY KE ZHICK 1/0/0/1 $6.75 #31
O WAW NE KE WAY 1/1/1/3 $20.25 #32
O NAY GISH 1/1/0/2 $13.50 #33
MAY ME GWE 1/1/1/3 $20.25 #34
WAIN GE ZHE YAW 1/1/4/6 $40.50 #35
A KEN 1/1/2/4 $27.00 #36
O GE MAW QUAY 0/1/0/1 $6.75 #37
CHE NE WAY 0/1/2/3 $20.25 #38
KAW KE, Joseph 1/0/0/1 $6.75 #39
MAW CHE WE TAW 1/1/4/6 $40.50 #40
WE ZO MO TAY 1/1/5/7 $47.25 #41
NAW NE ME NUCK SKUCK 1/1/4/6 $40.50 #42
PE QUAW KO SAY 1/1/1/3 $20.25 #43
MAW NE DO QUE WE SAUSE 1/1/4/6 $40.50 #44
SIN GO QUAY 0/1/1/2 $13.50 #45
MAW SO, Joseph 1/1/3/5 $33.75 #46
MIX, John 1/1/6/8 $54.00 #47
WAW SO 1/0/1/2 $13.50 #48
PAY ME KO WAY 1/1/0/2 $13.50 #49

1862 ANNUITY ROLL FOR YEAR
CHIPPEWA, OTTAWA & POTAWATOMI OF MICHIGAN

SIN GO WAW BAND

SIN GO WAW (Chief) 1/1/0/2 $12.80 #1
WAW GAW KO WE NAW, Mrs. 0/1/0/1 $6.40 #2
NAW O QUAY YAW 0/1/0/1 $6.40 #3
NAW O KEE 1/1/0/2 $12.80 #4
WAW O GIN 1/1/4/6 $38.40 #5
PAY CAW SAW 1/3/2/6 $38.40 #6
MICK SE MOCK 1/1/2/4 $25.60 #7
WAY ME GWAUSE 1/0/0/1 $6.40 #8

NAW KEE 1/1/2/4 $25.60 #9
SE THONE 1st 1/1/3/5 $32.00 #10
SE THONE 2nd 1/1/2/4 $25.60 #11
WILLIAM 1/1/2/4 $25.60 #12
KE CHE NAY GO 1/1/4/6 $38.40 #13
TE QUON 1/1/3/5 $32.00 #14
CHE CUSH CAW MO QUAY 0/1/3/4 $25.60 #15
WAW SAW TOE 1/0/1/2 $12.80 #16
JACKSON 1/0/0/1 $6.40 #17
AISH KE BE 1/1/1/3 $19.20 #18
O GE MAW WE 1/1/4/6 $38.40 #19
NAW TAW WAY WISH 1/1/0/2 $12.80 #20
WAUB SIGH 1/1/3/5 $32.00 #21
PARSONS, Mrs. Levi 0/1/7/8 $51.20 #22
QUAY GO NO 1/1/4/6 $38.40 #23
O SKE NAW WAY 1/1/4/6 $38.40 #24
SO ZETTE 0/1/1/2 $12.80 #25
BIG WE ZO 1/1/0/2 $12.80 #26
KAW O GO MO 1/1/0/2 $12.80 #27
KE ZHICK 1/1/0/2 $12.80 #28
WAW GAW KO ZHICK 1/0/0/1 $6.40 #29
TAY CAW MAW GAY 1/1/4/6 $38.40 #30
MAW CAW DAY KE ZHICK 1/0/0/1 $6.40 #31
O WAW NE KE WAY 1/1/1/3 $19.20 #32
O NAY GISH 1/1/0/2 $12.80 #33
MAY ME GWE 1/1/1/3 $19.20 #34
WAIN GE ZHE YAW 1/1/5/7 $44.80 #35
A KEN 1/1/3/5 $32.00 #36
O GE MAW QUAY 0/1/0/1 $6.40 #37
CHE NE WAY 0/1/2/3 $19.20 #38
KAW KEE, Joseph 1/0/0/1 $6.40 #39
MAW CHE WE TAW 1/1/3/5 $32.00 #40
WE ZO MO TAY 1/1/6/8 $51.20 #41
NAW NE ME NUCH SHUCK 1/1/4/6 $38.40 #42
PE QUAW KO SAY 1/1/1/3 $19.20 #43
MAW NE DO QUE WE SAUSE 1/1/4/6 $38.40 #44
SIN GO QUAY 0/1/1/2 $12.80 #45
MAW SO, Joseph 1/1/4/6 $38.40 #46
MIX, John 1/1/6/8 $51.20 #47
MAW SO 1/0/1/2 $12.80 #48
PAY ME KO WAY 1/1/1/3 $19.20 #49
NAW TAY MO QUAY 0/1/0/1 $6.40 #50

PO KAY GON BAND

PO KAY GON, Francis (Chief) 1/0/0/1 $6.40 #1
AW QUE WE NAW 2/2/4/8 $51.20 #2
PO KAY GON, James 1/0/1/2 $12.80 #3
AW SUCK 1/1/2/4 $25.60 #4
MOOSE 1/1/0/2 $12.80 #5

31

RAPP, Geo. 1/1/3/5 $32.00 #6
SAW GO SE MAW 1/1/4/6 $38.40 #7
PE MOW QUA NUM 0/1/3/4 $25.60 #8
AUGUSTUS, Wm. 1/1/3/5 $32.00 #9
AUGUSTUS, Mrs. Nich. 0/1/1/2 $12.80 #10
KAW KAW KAW SHE 1/0/5/6 $38.40 #11
RAIL, Mrs. Antoine 0/1/2/3 $19.20 #12
KEN NES QUAY'S Child 0/0/1/1 $6.40 #13
CUSHWAY, John 1/0/0/1 $6.40 #14
MAW NEE TO POSH 0/1/0/1 $6.40 #15
TO POSH, Mrs. 0/1/0/1 $6.40 #16
KE NO NAW NE QUAY 0/1/3/4 $25.60 #17
MAW SO 1/0/0/1 $6.40 #18
AW DAW QUAW NUM 0/1/0/1 $6.40 #19
SHE PE SHE WAW NO 1/1/1/3 $19.20 #20
SHAW WAW NAY SE 0/0/1/1 $6.40 #21

1863 ANNUITY ROLL FOR YEAR
CHIPPEWA, OTTAWA & POTAWATOMI OF MICHIGAN

SIN GO WAW BAND

SIN GO WAW (Chief) 1/1/0/2 $12.90 #1
PARSONS, Mrs. Levi 0/1/7/8 $51.60 #2
PAY CAW SAW 1/3/3/7 $45.15 #3
WAIN GE ZHE YAW 1/1/5/7 $45.15 #4
WEZO MOTAY 1/1/5/7 $45.15 #5
MIX, John 1/1/6/8 $51.60 #6
WAW O GIN 1/1/4/6 $38.70 #7
SETHONE 1st 1/1/4/6 $38.70 #8
KE CHE NAY GO 1/1/4/6 $38.70 #9
OGE MAW WE 1/1/4/6 $38.70 #10
WAUB SIGH 1/1/4/6 $38.70 #11
OSKE NAW WAY 1/1/4/6 $38.70 #12
TAY CAW MAW GAY 1/1/4/6 $38.70 #13
NAW NE ME NUCK SKUCK 1/1/4/6 $38.70 #14
MAWSO, Joseph 1/1/4/6 $38.70 #15
NAW KEE 1/1/3/5 $32.25 #16
TEQUON 1/1/3/5 $32.25 #17
QUAY GO NO 1/0/4/5 $32.25 #18
AKEN 1/1/3/5 $32.25 #19
MAW CHE WE TAW 1/1/3/5 $32.25 #20
MICK SE MOCK 1/1/2/4 $25.80 #21
SETHONE 2nd 1/1/2/4 $25.80 #22
WILLIAM 1/1/2/4 $25.80 #23
CHE CUSH CAW MO QUAY 0/1/3/4 $25.80 #24
MAW NE DO QUE WE SAUSE 1/1/2/4 $25.80 #25
WAW SAW TOE 1/0/2/3 $19.35 #26
AISH KE BE 1/1/1/3 $19.35 #27

32

O WAW NE KE WAY 1/1/1/3 $19.35 #28
MAY WE GWE 1/1/1/3 $19.35 #29
CHE NE WAY 0/1/2/3 $19.35 #30
PE QUAW KO SAY 1/1/1/3 $19.35 #31
NAW OKEE 1/1/0/2 $12.90 #32
SAW GE MAW QUAY 0/1/1/2 $12.90 #33
SOZETTE 0/1/1/2 $12.90 #34
KE CHE WE ZO 1/1/0/2 $12.90 #35
KAW OGO MO 1/1/0/2 $12.90 #36
KEZHICK 1/1/0/2 $12.90 #37
O NAY GISH 1/1/0/2 $12.90 #38
SIN GO QUAY 0/1/1/2 $12.90 #39
WAW GAW KO WE NAW 0/1/0/1 $6.45 #40
NAW O QUAY YAW 0/1/0/1 $6.45 #41
JACKSON 1/0/0/1 $6.45 #42
WAW GAW KEZHICK 1/0/0/1 $6.45 #43
OGE MAW QUAY 0/1/0/1 $6.45 #44
KAW KEE, Joseph 1/0/0/1 $6.45 #45
MARY 0/1/0/1 $6.45 #46
BATTISE, John 1/0/0/1 $6.45 #47
WAW SO 1/0/0/1 $6.45 #48
KAW BAISH CAW MO QUAY 0/1/0/1 $6.45 #49
NAW TAY MO QUAY 0/1/0/1 $6.45 #50
MAW CAW DAY KEZHICK 1/0/0/1 $6.45 #51

PO KAY GON BAND

PO KAY GON, Francis (Chief) 1/0/0/1 $6.45 #1
AW QUE WE NAW 2/2/4/8 $51.60 #2
KAW KAW KAW SHE 1/0/6/7 $45.15 #3
SAW GO SE MAW 1/1/4/6 $38.70 #4
RAPP, Geo. 1/1/4/6 $38.70 #5
AUGUSTUS, Wm. 1/1/3/5 $32.25 #6
AW SUCK 1/1/2/4 $25.80 #7
PE WAW QUO NUM 0/1/3/4 $25.80 #8
KEY NO NAW NE QUAY 0/1/3/4 $25.80 #9
RAIL, Mrs. Antoine 0/1/2/3 $19.35 #10
SHEPE SHE WAW NO 1/1/1/3 $19.35 #11
PO KAY GON, James 1/0/1/2 $12.90 #12
MOOSE 1/1/0/2 $12.90 #13
SINNESEQUAY'S Child 0/0/1/1 $6.45 #14
CUSHWAY, John 1/0/0/1 $6.45 #15
MAW NE TO POSH 0/1/0/1 $6.45 #16
TOPOSH, Mrs. 0/1/0/1 $6.45 #17
MAW SO 1/0/0/1 $6.45 #18
AW DAW QUAW NUM 0/1/0/1 $6.45 #19
SHAW WAW MAYSE 0/0/1/1 $6.45 #20

33

SIN GO WAW BAND

SIN GO WAW (Chief) 1/1/0/2 $10.22 #1
WEZO MOTAY 1/1/6/8 $40.88 #2
MIX, John 1/1/6/8 $40.88 #3
WAIN GE SHE YAW 1/1/5/7 $35.77 #4
PARSONS, Mrs. Levi 0/1/5/6 $30.66 #5
WAW O GIN 1/1/4/6 $30.66 #6
SETHONE 1st 1/1/4/6 $30.66 #7
KE CHE NAY GO 1/1/4/6 $30.66 #8
OGEMAW WE 1/1/4/6 $30.66 #9
WAUB SIGH 1/1/4/6 $30.66 #10
OSKE NAW WAY 1/1/4/6 $30.66 #11
NAW NE ME NUCK SKUCK 1/1/4/6 $30.66 #12
MAWSO, Joseph 1/1/4/6 $30.66 #13
QUAY GO MO 1/1/4/6 $30.66 #14
TAY CAW MAW GAY 1/1/3/5 $25.55 #15
NAW GEE 1/1/3/5 $25.55 #16
TE QUON 1/1/3/5 $25.55 #17
AKEN 1/1/3/5 $25.55 #18
WILLIAM 1/1/3/5 $25.55 #19
MAW CHE WETAW 1/1/2/4 $20.44 #20
MICK SE MOCK 1/1/2/4 $20.44 #21
SETHONE 2nd 1/1/2/4 $20.44 #22
CHE CUSH CAW MO QUAY 0/1/3/4 $20.44 #23
MAW NE DO QUE WE SAUSE 1/1/2/4 $20.44 #24
ME SQUAW BAW NO QUAY 0/1/2/3 $15.33 #25
AISH KEBE 1/1/1/3 $15.33 #26
ONAW NEKE WAY 1/1/1/3 $15.33 #27
MAY ME GWE 1/1/1/3 $15.33 #28
CHE NE WAY 0/1/2/3 $15.33 #29
PE QUAW CO SAY 1/1/1/3 $15.33 #30
PAY CAW SAW 1/1/0/2 $10.22 #31
WEZO, Louis 1/1/0/2 $10.22 #32
KEZHE GO QUAY 0/1/1/2 $10.22 #33
WAW SACO TOE 1/0/1/2 $10.22 #34
NAW OKEE 1/1/0/2 $10.22 #35
SOZETTE 0/1/1/2 $10.22 #36
KECHE WEZO 1/1/0/2 $10.22 #37
KAW OGO MO 1/1/0/2 $10.22 #38
KEZHICK 1/1/0/2 $10.22 #39
SIN GO QUAY 0/1/1/2 $10.22 #40
BATTISE, John 1/0/1/2 $10.22 #41
SAW GE MAW QUAY 0/1/0/1 $5.11 #42
MAISH QUOS 0/1/0/1 $5.11 #43
WAW GAW CO WE NAW, Mrs. 0/1/0/1 $5.11 #44
NAW O QUAY YAW 0/1/0/1 $5.11 #45

JACKSON 1/0/0/1 $5.11 #46
WAW GAW KO ZHICK 1/0/0/1 $5.11 #47
OGE MAW QUAY 0/1/0/1 $5.11 #48
KAW KEE, Jos. 1/0/0/1 $5.11 #49
MARY 0/1/0/1 $5.11 #50
WAW SO 1/0/0/1 $5.11 #51
WAW KAY SE NO QUAY 0/1/0/1 $5.11 #52
SIN GO WAW, Elizabeth 0/1/0/1 $5.11 #53
SIN GO WAW, Elizabeth (Infant) 0/0/1/1 $5.11 #54

POKAYGON BAND

POKAYGON, Francis (Chief) 1/0/0/1 $5.11 #1
AW QUE WE NAW 2/2/4/8 $40.88 #2
KAW KAW KAW SHE 1/0/6/7 $35.77 #3
RAPP, Geo. 1/1/4/6 $30.66 #4
AUGUSTUS, Wm. 1/1/4/6 $30.66 #5
SAW GO SE MAW 1/1/3/5 $25.55 #6
KE NO NAW NE QUAY 0/1/3/4 $20.44 #7
MARY 0/1/2/3 $15.33 #8
PE WAW QUO OM 0/1/2/3 $15.33 #9
RAIL, Mrs. Ant. 0/1/2/3 $15.33 #10
SHE PE SHE WAW NO 1/1/1/3 $15.33 #11
POKAYGON, Jas. 1/0/1/2 $10.22 #12
MOOSE 1/1/0/2 $10.22 #13
ANSE, Mrs. Auth. 0/1/0/1 $5.11 #14
CUSHWAY, John 1/0/0/1 $5.11 #15
MAWNE POTOSH 0/1/0/1 $5.11 #16
POTOSH, Mrs. 0/1/0/1 $5.11 #17
MAW SO 1/0/0/1 $5.11 #18
SHAW WAW NAY SE 1/0/0/1 $5.11 #19

1865 ANNUITY ROLL FOR YEAR
CHIPPEWA, OTTAWA & POTAWATOMI OF MICHIGAN

SIN GO WAW BAND

SIN GO WAW (Chief) 1/1/0/2 $19.50 #1
MIX, John 1/1/6/8 $78.00 #2
WAIN GE ZHE AW 1/1/5/7 $68.25 #3
QUAY GO NO 1/1/5/7 $68.25 #4
WEZO MOTAY 1/1/4/6 $58.50 #5
WAW O GIN 1/1/4/6 $58.50 #6
SETHONE 1st 1/1/4/6 $58.50 #7
KE CHE NAY GO 1/1/4/6 $58.50 #8
OGE MAW WE 1/1/4/6 $58.50 #9
WAUB SIGH 1/1/4/6 $58.50 #10
OSKE NAW WAY 1/1/4/6 $58.50 #11
NAW NE ME NUCK SKUCK 1/1/4/6 $58.50 #12

35

MAWSO, Joseph 1/1/4/6 $58.50 #13
TAY CAW MAW GAY 1/1/3/5 $48.75 #14
AKEN 1/1/3/5 $48.75 #15
WILLIAM 1/1/3/5 $48.75 #16
MAW NE DO QUE WE SAUSE 1/1/3/5 $48.75 #17
SETHONE 2nd 1/1/3/5 $48.75 #18
PARSONS, Mrs. Levi 0/1/3/4 $39.00 #19
NAW GEE, Marion 0/1/3/4 $39.00 #20
TE QUON 1/1/2/4 $39.00 #21
MAW CHE WE TAW 1/1/2/4 $39.00 #22
MICK SE MOCK 1/1/2/4 $39.00 #23
ME SQUAW BAW NO QUAY 0/1/2/3 $29.25 #24
AISH KE BE 1/1/1/3 $29.25 #25
O WAW NE KE WAY 1/1/1/3 $29.25 #26
MAY ME GWE 1/1/1/3 $29.25 #27
CHE NE WAY 0/1/2/3 $29.25 #28
PE QUAW CO SAY 1/1/1/3 $29.25 #29
KAW O GO MO 1/1/1/3 $29.25 #30
PAY CAW SAY 1/1/0/2 $19.50 #31
WEZO, Louis 1/1/0/2 $19.50 #32
WAW SAW TOE 1/0/1/2 $19.50 #33
NAW OKEE 1/1/0/2 $19.50 #34
SOZETTE 0/1/1/2 $19.50 #35
KE CHE WEZO 1/1/0/2 $19.50 #36
KE ZHICK 1/1/0/2 $19.50 #37
SIN GO QUAY 0/1/1/2 $19.50 #38
KE ZHE GO QUAY 0/1/0/1 $9.75 #39
BATTISE, John 1/0/0/1 $9.75 #40
KEY TOSH 1/0/0/1 $9.75 #41
SAW GE MAW QUAY 0/1/0/1 $9.75 #42
MAISH QUOS 0/1/0/1 $9.75 #43
WAW GAW KO WE NAW 0/1/0/1 $9.75 #44
JACKSON 1/0/0/1 $9.75 #45
WAW GAW KO ZHICK 1/0/0/1 $9.75 #46
OGE MAW QUAY 0/1/0/1 $9.75 #47
KAWKEE, Joseph 1/0/0/1 $9.75 #48
BERTRAND, Mary 0/1/0/1 $9.75 #49
WAW SO 1/0/0/1 $9.75 #50
WAW KAY SE NO QUAY 0/1/0/1 $9.75 #51
SINGOWAW, Elizabeth 0/1/0/1 $9.75 #52

POKAYGON BAND

POKAYGON, Francis (Chief) 1/0/0/1 $9.75 #1
AW QUE WE NAW 1/1/5/7 $68.25 #2
KAW KAW KE SHE 1/0/6/7 $68.25 #3
RAPP, Geo. 1/1/5/7 $68.25 #4
AUGUSTUS, Wm. 1/1/4/6 $58.50 #5
SAW GO SE MAW 1/1/4/6 $58.50 #6
KE NO NAW NE QUAY 0/1/3/4 $39.00 #7

36

PAY SHE WAY, Mary 0/1/2/3 $29.25 #8
PE WAW QUO NUM 0/1/2/3 $29.25 #9
RAIL, Mrs. Ant. 0/1/2/3 $29.25 #10
SHE PE SHE WAW NO 1/1/1/3 $29.35 #11
POKAYGON, James 1/0/1/2 $19.50 #12
DOMINEKE 1/0/0/1 $9.75 #13
MOOSE 1/0/0/1 $9.75 #14
ANSE, Mrs. Antome 0/1/0/1 $9.75 #15
CUSHWAY, John 1/0/0/1 $9.75 #16
MAWNE TOPOSH 0/1/0/1 $9.75 #17
TOPOSH, Mrs. 0/1/0/1 $9.75 #18

1866 ANNUITY ROLL FOR YEAR
CHIPPEWA, OTTAWA & POTAWATOMI OF MICHIGAN

SIN GO WAW (Chief) 1/1/0/2 $339.00 #1
MIX, John 1/1/6/8 $1,356.00 #2
WAIN GE ZHE YAW 1/1/5/7 $1,186.50 #3
QUAY GO NO 1/1/5/7 $1,186.50 #4
WAUB SIGH 1/1/5/7 $1,186.50 #5
O SKE NAW WAY 1/1/5/7 $1,186.50 #6
KAW KAW KAW SHE 1/0/6/7 $1,186.50 #7
RAPP, George 1/1/5/7 $1,186.50 #8
WE ZO MOTAY 1/1/4/6 $1,017.00 #9
WAW O GIN 1/1/4/6 $1,017.00 #10
KECHE SETHONE 1/1/4/6 $1,017.00 #11
KE CHE NAY GO 1/1/4/6 $1,017.00 #12
O GE MAW WE 1/1/4/6 $1,017.00 #13
MAWSO, Joseph 1/1/4/6 $1,017.00 #14
AKEN 1/1/4/6 $1,017.00 #15
WILLIAM 1/1/4/6 $1,017.00 #16
PARSONS, Mrs. Levi 0/1/5/6 $1,017.00 #17
AW QUE WE NAW 0/1/5/6 $1,017.00 #18
AUGUSTUS, William 1/1/4/6 $1,017.00 #19
PO KAY GON, Simon 1/1/4/6 $1,017.00 #20
O SAW GE QUAY 0/1/4/5 $847.50 #21
TAY CAW MAW GAY 1/1/3/5 $847.50 #22
SETHONE 2nd 1/1/3/5 $847.50 #23
PO KAY GON, James 1/1/3/5 $847.50 #24
MAW NE DO GWE WE SAUSE 1/1/2/4 $678.00 #25
NAW GEE, Marion 0/1/3/4 $678.00 #26
TE QUON 1/1/2/4 $678.00 #27
MICK SE MOCK 1/1/2/4 $678.00 #28
KE NO NAW NE QUAY 0/1/3/4 $678.00 #29
MAW CHE WE TAW 1/1/1/3 $508.50 #30
ME SQUAW BAW NO QUAY 0/1/2/3 $508.50 #31
AISH KE BE 1/1/1/3 $508.50 #32
MAY ME GWE 1/1/1/3 $508.50 #33
PE QUAW CO SAY 1/1/1/3 $508.50 #34

37

KAW O GO MO 1/1/1/3 $508.50 #35
KEY TOSH 1/1/1/3 $508.50 #36
RAIL, Antoine 0/1/2/3 $508.50 #37
KE NE SO QUAY 0/1/1/2 $339.00 #38
PAY CO SAW 0/1/1/2 $339.00 #39
WEZO, Louis 1/1/0/2 $339.00 #40
NAW O KEE 1/1/0/2 $339.00 #41
SO ZETTE 0/1/1/2 $339.00 #42
KE CHE WE ZO 1/1/0/2 $339.00 #43
KE ZHICK 1/1/0/2 $339.00 #44
SIN GO QUAY 0/1/1/2 $339.00 #45
BAZIL, Mary 0/1/1/2 $339.00 #46
PE WAW QUO NUM 0/1/1/2 $339.00 #47
BAZIL, John 1/1/0/2 $339.00 #48
PO KAY GON, Lawrence 1/1/0/2 $339.00 #49
PO KAY GON, Francis (Chief) 1/0/0/1 $169.50 #50
DOMINEKE 1/0/0/1 $169.50 #51
MOOSE 1/0/0/1 $169.50 #52
ANSE, Mrs. Antoine 0/1/0/1 $169.50 #53
CUSHWAY, John 1/0/0/1 $169.50 #54
MAWNEE TOPOSH 0/1/0/1 $169.50 #55
AUGUSTUS, Louis 1/0/0/1 $169.50 #56
BATTISE, Peter 1/0/0/1 $169.50 #57
BATTISE, John 1/0/0/1 $169.50 #58
SAW GO MAW QUAY 0/1/0/1 $169.50 #59
MAISH QUOS 0/1/0/1 $169.50 #60
WAW GO KO WE NAW, Mrs. 0/1/0/1 $169.50 #61
JACKSON 1/0/0/1 $169.50 #62
O GE MAW QUAY 0/1/0/1 $169.50 #63
KAW KEE, Joseph 1/0/0/1 $169.50 #64
WAW SO 1/0/0/1 $169.50 #65
SIN GO WAW, Elizabeth 0/1/0/1 $169.50 #66
WAW SAW TOE 1/0/0/1 $169.50 #67

1869 ANNUITY ROLL FOR 3RD QTR
POTTAWATOMI OF INDIANA & MICHIGAN

A-COB-WAH-PORCH 1/0/0/1 $12.00
A-DUWA-DUK 1/0/0/1 $12.00
A-KE-O-KO-WA 0/0/1/1 $12.00
ACTON, Angeline 0/0/5/5 $60.00
ACTON, Madeline 0/0/6/6 $72.00
AH-GOT 0/1/2/3 $36.00
AH-ZAH-NAH-BE 0/0/1/1 $12.00
AHB-TWA-KE-ZHICK 1/0/1/2 $24.00
AHB-TWE-TUK 1/0/2/3 $36.00
AHCH-MAH-GWE 1/0/0/1 $12.00
AHLE-NAHB 1/0/0/1 $12.00
AHN-BE-AS 0/0/2/2 $24.00

AHN-NEB-LEA 0/0/4/4 $48.00
AHN-ZHE-WA 1/1/2/4 $48.00
AHZH-NICK 0/0/2/2 $24.00
ALLEY, Saml. 0/0/1/1 $12.00
AMAB-TUPIN 0/0/5/5 $60.00
AN-WAH-BA 1/1/4/6 $72.00
ANDERSON, John 0/0/4/4 $48.00
ANDERSON, Peter 1/0/0/1 $12.00
ARCHANGE (Nolin) 0/1/0/1 $12.00
ASHMORE, Mary 0/0/1/1 $12.00
B-GO-GUO-QUA 0/0/3/3 $36.00
BABEAU, Archange 0/0/2/2 $24.00
BALDAN, James 0/0/4/4 $48.00
BASIL 1/0/1/2 $36.00
BAYLESS, Almira 0/1/2/3 $36.00
BEAUBIEN, Edward 0/0/2/2 $24.00
BEAUBIEN, Lydia 0/0/2/2 $24.00
BEAUBIEN, M. B. 0/0/4/4 $48.00
BEHAN, Patrick 0/0/4/4 $48.00
BERGERON, Francis 0/0/1/1 $12.00
BERTRAND, Adalaide 1/0/0/1 $12.00
BERTRAND, J. H. 0/0/3/3 $36.00
BERTRAND, Joseph Henry 1/0/0/1 $12.00
BERTRAND, B. B. 0/0/2/2 $24.00
BERTRAND, B. H. 0/0/2/2 $24.00
BERTRAND, Henrietta 0/1/0/1 $12.00
BERTRAND, Joseph 0/0/4/4 $48.00
BERTRAND, Paul 1/0/0/1 $12.00
BLACK HAWK 1/1/6/8 $96.00
BLACK JOE 1/0/0/1 $12.00
BLACKBIRD, Louis 0/0/3/3 $36.00
BLIND MAN 2/0/0/2 $24.00
BOATMAN, John 0/0/1/1 $12.00
BONESE, Peter 0/0/3/3 $36.00
BONIES 0/0/1/1 $12.00
BOSTIC, David 0/0/2/2 $24.00
BOURASSA, DAVID 0/1/0/1 $12.00
BOURASSA, Thos. 0/0/2/2 $24.00
BOURASSA, Alex 0/0/1/1 $12.00
BOURASSA, Theodore 1/0/0/1 $12.00
BOURASSA, Eugine 1/1/4/6 $72.00
BOURASSA, Joseph N. 0/1/7/8 $96.00
BOURBONAIS, Frank 0/0/1/1 $12.00
BOURBONAIS, Frank 1/1/6/8 $96.00
BOURBONIC, Mary 0/1/8/9 $108.00
BOURBONIC, Anthony 0/0/4/4 $48.00
BOURDON, Judith 0/2/4/6 $72.00
BOURDON, Judith 0/0/1/1 $12.00
BROWN, Wm. 1/0/0/1 $12.00
BRUNO, Baptiste 0/1/2/3 $36.00

39

BURKE, Joe 0/0/1/1 $12.00
BURNETT, A. B. 0/0/7/7 $84.00
BZ-HICH-KEES 0/0/3/3 $36.00
CANADA, Madeline 0/1/0/1 $12.00
CATICK, John 0/1/0/1 $12.00
CE-NAHS, John 0/0/2/2 $24.00
CHAH-CAH-BE 0/0/3/3 $36.00
CHAPPUE, Joseph 1/2/2/5 $60.00
CHAPPUE, Frank 1/0/0/1 $12.00
CHE-GWES 1/0/0/1 $12.00
CHE-QUAH-KE-AH 0/0/3/3 $36.00
CHEMON, Louise 0/0/3/3 $36.00
CHI-COP-KIS-SA 1/1/1/3 $36.00
CHICK-SAW 0/0/1/1 $12.00
CLARDY, J. E. 0/0/5/5 $60.00
CLARK, Mrs. S. W. 0/0/3/3 $36.00
CLARK, L. W. 0/0/1/1 $12.00
COLD 0/1/3/4 $48.00
CONTRAMAN, Jacob 1/0/0/1 $12.00
COON, Solomon 0/0/1/1 $12.00
CROW, Jim 1/0/0/1 $12.00
CUMMINGS, Saml. 0/1/5/6 $72.00
CURLY, Antoine 0/0/2/2 $24.00
DARLING, L. R. 0/0/3/3 $36.00
DARLING, Frank 0/0/1/1 $12.00
DEAN, Charles 0/0/3/3 $36.00
DEGRAFF, John 0/0/5/5 $60.00
DEHONEY, Zoe 0/1/1/2 $24.00
DELONG, Havier 0/0/1/1 $12.00
DEROSIER, Lezette 0/0/2/2 $24.00
DIKE, Reason 0/0/3/3 $36.00
E-DWE-E-ZE 0/0/1/1 $12.00
E-TWEH-E 1/0/0/1 $12.00
EASTON, D. F. 0/0/2/2 $24.00
EAT-ALL 1/3/14/18 $216.00
ED-WA-GE-ZHICK 0/0/3/3 $36.00
ED-WAH-GE-ZHICK 0/0/4/4 $48.00
ELLIOT, Sophronia 0/0/1/1 $12.00
EM-QUAHN 0/0/2/2 $24.00
ETTIENNE 1/0/0/1 $12.00
EVANS, Thos. 0/0/3/3 $36.00
EVANS, Joseph 0/0/1/1 $12.00
FIELDS, Saml. 2/0/0/2 $24.00
FORD, Henry 0/0/2/2 $24.00
FOUR FACED 1/0/0/1 $12.00
FRAPP, Gabe 0/0/2/2 $24.00
FREGO, Hillary 0/0/1/1 $12.00
FREGON, Margaret 0/0/1/1 $12.00
FRERE, Frank 0/0/2/2 $24.00
FULLER, Louis 0/0/1/1 $12.00

GA-GAH-DMO 0/0/4/4/ $48.00
GHE-GE-AHK 0/1/0/1 $12.00
GOSLIN, Lizette 0/0/1/1 $12.00
GOSLIN, Antoine 0/1/3/4 $48.00
GREEMORE, Mrs. 0/0/4/4 $48.00
GREEMORE, Joseph 0/0/4/4 $48.00
GREEN, David 0/0/2/2 $24.00
GREEN, Frank 0/0/1/1 $12.00
HAAS, Ruebin 0/1/3/4 $48.00
HALE, John 0/0/2/2 $24.00
HALF DAY 1/0/0/1 $12.00
HARDIN, John 0/0/5/5 $60.00
HASCALL, Thos. 0/0/2/2 $24.00
HERD, John 0/0/2/2 $24.00
HIGBEE, Alva 0/0/6/6 $72.00
HOOVER, Michael 0/0/3/3 $36.00
I-O-MA-QUA 0/0/1/1 $12.00
I-OT-KA 0/1/0/1 $12.00
IGNATIUS 1/0/0/1 $12.00
JACKSON, Mrs. 0/0/2/2 $24.00
JOHNSON, Jacob 0/0/4/4 $48.00
JOHNSON, James 0/0/2/2 $24.00
JOT-TOSE 0/1/3/4 $48.00
JUNEAU, N. M. 0/1/4/5 $60.00
KA-BAM-SA, Ann 0/0/4/4 $48.00
KA-CAM-ME 1/1/0/2 $24.00
KA-KE-MEKAS 0/1/1/2 $24.00
KAH-BATCH 1/0/1/2 $24.00
KAH-DAH-DUS 0/1/5/6 $72.00
KAH-DOT (Old) 0/0/3/3 $36.00
KAH-KA-OSA 1/0/0/1 $12.00
KAH-KA-QUA-BE 1/0/0/1 $12.00
KAH-KAS 0/0/1/1 $12.00
KAH-O-ZO-QUA 0/0/1/1 $12.00
KAH-OTAH-KE-ZHICK 1/1/2/4 $48.00
KAKE-CAKE 1/0/1/2 $24.00
KAP-SEO-WID 0/1/3/4 $48.00
KE-O-KUM 1/0/0/1 $12.00
KE-SIS 1/0/0/1 $12.00
KE-WA-SA 0/1/3/4 $48.00
KE-WAN-KA 0/2/0/2 $24.00
KE-WAT-NE-UM, Paul 1/0/0/1 $12.00
KEMP, Elnora 0/1/1/2 $24.00
KEN-WAHN-NO 1/1/4/6 $72.00
KENEDY, Jane 0/0/1/1 $12.00
KENNADY, Ephrium 0/1/7/8 $96.00
KESH-GOSE 1/0/0/1 $12.00
KESH-QUE 1/0/0/1 $12.00
KEW-ME-KAS 0/0/1/1 $12.00
KO-TOSE 1/0/0/1 $12.00

KOSH-QUA (Greasy) 1/0/0/1 $12.00
KOSH-QUA (Pe-was) 1/0/0/1 $12.00
KUK-JISE 1/1/3/5 $60.00
LA FROMBOISE, Cecile 0/1/0/1 $12.00
LA CLERE, John 0/0/3/3 #36.00
LAFROMBOISE, Therese 0/0/2/2 $24.00
LAFROMBOISE, Francis 1/1/3/5 $60.00
LAFROMBOISE, 0/0/2/2 $24.00
LAFROMBOISE, Catharine 0/1/3/4 $48.00
LAPOINTE, Alex. 1/0/0/1 $12.00
LASLEY, J. D. 0/0/6/6 $72.00
LASLEY, John Jr. 1/0/0/1 $12.00
LAZZELL, Thos. 0/0/4/4 $48.00
LAZZELL, Wm. 0/0/1/1 $12.00
LE CLERE, Peter 0/0/5/5 $60.00
LE CLERE 1/1/2/4 $48.00
LE MOUNTAINE, Edward 0/0/2/2 $24.00
LE CLERE, Frank 1/1/2/4 $48.00
LETENDRE, John 1/1/0/2 $24.00
LEVIA, Mary 0/1/1/2 $24.00
LEVIA, James 0/0/2/2 $24.00
LEWIS, Wesley 0/0/2/2 $24.00
LEWIS, Wesley 0/0/1/1 $12.00
LITTLE AMERICAN 0/1/0/1 $12.00
LITTLE WOLF 1/0/0/1 $12.00
LONGHAIR, John B. 1/1/2/4 $48.00
LUCIER, William 0/0/1/1
MA-MOS-KE 0/0/1/1 $12.00
MA-NA-WUK 1/1/4/6 $72.00
MA-TAHK-SA 0/1/1/2 $24.00
MA-WAH 0/0/1/1 $12.00
MA-ZAH-ONAH 2/0/1/3 $36.00
MA-ZAH-ONAH (Halfday) 0/0/1/1 $12.00
MA-ZHE 0/0/2/2 $24.00
MA-ZHOS 1/1/4/6 $72.00
MACK-TA-O-SHIG 1/1/3/5 $60.00
MAH-CHE-WAS 0/0/1/1 $12.00
MAH-JWAS 0/4/0/4 $48.00
MAH-JWAS 0/0/2/2 $24.00
MAH-NE-AN-WISH-MAH 0/0/1/1 $12.00
MAH-SHA, Francis 1/1/0/2 $24.00
MAH-TE-NAN 0/0/1/1 $12.00
MAHK-SID 1/1/1/3 $36.00
MALOCH, Joseph 1/1/1/3 $36.00
MAN-PO-AH 0/1/0/1 $12.00
MAN-PO-AH 0/1/0/1 $12.00
MANN, Peter 0/0/2/2 $24.00
MANN, Peter Jr. 0/0/1/1 $12.00
MARANDAT, Louise 0/1/0/1 $12.00
MARANDOT, Josette 1/1/0/2 $24.00

MARSHALL 0/1/0/1 $12.00
MARTEL, Wm. 0/0/9/9 $108.00
MAS-QUAS 1/1/4/6 $72.00
MASH-KEA-SHUCK 2/0/0/2 $24.00
MAT-SAP-TO 1/1/1/3 $36.00
MAT-WAS 1/1/7/9 $108.00
MATCH-KE 1/0/0/1 $12.00
MCA-TO-O-SHUK 1/0/0/1 $12.00
MCCARTNEY, Thomas 0/0/1/1 $12.00
MCFARLAND, Samuel 0/0/1/1 $12.00
MCKINNEY, Thos. L. 0/0/5/5 $60.00
MCLAIN, Albert 1/0/0/1 $12.00
MCPHERSON, Nelson 1/0/0/1 $12.00
MDA-O-MAG 0/0/2/2 $24.00
MDAH-ZAH 0/0/1/1 $12.00
MDWA-GE-WUN 0/1/1/2 $24.00
ME-AN-CO 0/0/3/3 $36.00
ME-GAH 0/0/2/2 $24.00
ME-SAH-GAH 1/0/0/1 $12.00
ME-SHAHS, Madeline 0/1/0/1 $12.00
ME-ZHAN-QUA 1/2/0/3 $36.00
MERRITT, J. S. 0/0/2/2 $24.00
MILOT, Joseph 0/0/1/1 $12.00
MILOT, Claude 0/0/5/5 $60.00
MIS-SAH-GE-QUA 0/1/1/2 $24.00
MISH-NO 2/0/0/2 $24.00
MJIH-QUES 0/0/3/3 $36.00
MJO-QUIS 1/0/0/1 $12.00
MKAH-DA-MOI 1/0/4/5 $60.00
MKO-PIN 1/0/0/1 $12.00
MKOM-DA 0/0/4/4 $48.00
MKUH-DA-MKO-QUA 2/1/0/3 $36.00
MKUH-DA-MWA 1/1/0/2 $24.00
MNIS-NO-CO-MAH 1/0/0/1 $12.00
MNIS-NO-OGIH-WAH 1/1/2/4 $48.00
MNIS-NO-QUA 0/0/2/2 $24.00
MNIS-NONE-SE 1/1/3/5 $60.00
MNIS-NONE-SE 0/1/3/4 $48.00
MO-NA 1/1/4/6 $72.00
MO-SAH-DUM 0/0/2/2 $24.00
MO-WA-TAH 0/2/0/2 $24.00
MO-WAS 1/1/2/4 $48.00
MOAN-KAH 1/1/3/5 $60.00
MOOSE, Peter 0/0/1/1 $12.00
MOOSE, Peter 0/0/1/1 $12.00
MOS-SWA 0/1/0/1 $12.00
MOSE 1/0/0/1 $12.00
MOZO-BANET, Joseph 1/1/1/3 $36.00
MOZO-BANET 0/0/3/3 $36.00
MSHA-WA-QUA 1/0/1/2 $24.00

MSHUK-NO-UK 1/0/0/1 $12.00
MSQUAHB-NO-QUA 0/1/0/1 $12.00
MSUCK-GAH-WE 1/0/0/1 $12.00
MTA-GOSE 0/1/1/2 $24.00
MTAH-MA 0/0/5/5 $60.00
MUC-COSE 1/1/3/5 $60.00
MUI-DO-MAG 1/1/0/2 $24.00
MULLER, Margaret 0/1/0/1 $12.00
MULLER, Jas. B. 1/0/0/1 $12.00
MULLER, George 1/0/0/1 $12.00
MUN-NO-MNE-QUA 1/1/3/5 $60.00
MUROE, Frank 0/0/1/1 $12.00
MUSH-CO 1/0/0/1 $12.00
MWA-TAH 0/1/1/2 $24.00
MYERS, John 0/0/1/1 $12.00
NA-CHE-WA 0/1/2/3 $36.00
NA-O-GWE 1/0/0/1 $12.00
NA-SWID-NO-QUA 0/1/0/1 $12.00
NA-TAH-GWA-TUK 1/0/0/1 $12.00
NADEAU, P. Alex 0/0/3/3 $36.00
NADEAU, Eli G. 1/1/8/10 $120.00
NAH-BA-DE 1/0/0/1 $12.00
NAH-DA-QUA 0/0/1/1 $12.00
NAH-MAHT-AHKUK 0/0/2/2 $24.00
NAH-NIM-NUK-SHKUK 0/0/2/2 $24.00
NAH-NIN-NUK-SHKUK 0/0/1/1 $12.00
NAH-ZHE 1/0/2/3 $36.00
NAHG-DO-NUK 1/1/5/7 $84.00
NAHK-SA 1/1/5/7 $84.00
NAK-KE 1/1/0/2 $24.00
NAM-SWE 1/1/4/6 $72.00
NAN-WAH-GA 1/0/0/1 $12.00
NANGO 1/0/2/3 $36.00
NASH-KA-OBE 1/0/1/2 $24.00
NAVARRE, Peter 0/0/6/6 $72.00
NAVARRE, Antoine 0/0/4/4 $48.00
NE-AHS 0/1/3/4 $48.00
NE-GAHN-GESH-GO-QUA 0/1/1/2 $24.00
NE-GAHN-KO-UK 1/0/0/1 $12.00
NE-GAHN-KO-UK 0/0/2/2 $24.00
NE-LEAH-QUAH 0/0/1/1 $12.00
NEAHS-PES-QUA-GE 1/0/2/3 $36.00
NEALY, John 0/1/3/4 $48.00
NO-NA 1/0/0/1 $12.00
NO-TAK-SA 0/1/1/2 $24.00
NON-EM-NUK-SHKUK 1/1/0/2 $24.00
NOTCH-WON-O-QUA 0/1/2/3 $36.00
NOW-GE-ZHICK (Mnuk-quet) 1/1/1/3 $36.00
NOW-GE-ZHICK 0/0/5/5 $60.00
NOW-QUA 1/1/2/4 $48.00

44

NOX-SA 0/0/5/5 $60.00
NSO-WAH-QUET 0/0/2/2 $24.00
NUEAK-TO (Hairlip) 1/1/1/3 $36.00
NUM-KESE 0/0/1/1 $12.00
NWA-KTO, Joe 0/1/1/2 $24.00
NWA-YAH-KOSE (Lame) 2/0/1/3 $36.00
NWA-ZAH-KO-SE 0/0/1/1 $12.00
NWAH-GA 0/0/1/1 $12.00
O-CHE-QUA 0/0/3/3 $36.00
O-CO-MAH-OSUM 1/0/0/1 $12.00
O-JE-QUA 1/1/3/5 $60.00
O-KETCH-KUM-ME 0/0/1/1 $12.00
O-PE-WAS 1/0/0/1 $12.00
O-SAH-WAH 0/2/0/2 $24.00
O-SAW-O-DIP 0/0/1/1 $12.00
O-SHEG-KE 0/1/0/1 $12.00
O-SKEN-MA 0/0/0/4 $48.00
O-TEN-O-QUA 0/1/1/2 $24.00
OBRIEN, Tim 0/0/5/5 $60.00
OGEE, L. H. 0/1/6/7 $84.00
OGEE, John 0/0/5/5 $60.00
OP-TE-GE-ZHICK 1/1/1/3 $36.00
OS-MID 0/0/1/1 $12.00
OS-MIT 0/0/3/3 $36.00
OZ-AH-O-MUK 0/1/2/3 $36.00
P___-DOSH 0/0/2/2 $24.00
PA-KTIN-MAH-GEN 1/0/0/1 $12.00
PA-MA 1/0/1/2 $24.00
PA-MAH-ME 0/0/4/4 $48.00
PA-MAW-KA-DUK 0/0/1/1 $12.00
PA-MOS-KA 1/1/7/9 $108.00
PA-MOS-KA-QUA 0/0/2/2 $24.00
PACK-CO-JA-BE (Young) 1/0/0/1 $12.00
PADE-GO-DO 1/0/0/1 $12.00
PAH-SO 0/0/1/1 $12.00
PAHIES 0/0/5/5 $60.00
PAHK-TGO 0/0/2/2 $24.00
PAKEKJA-BE 1/1/5/7 $84.00
PALMER, A. E. 0/0/1/1 $12.00
PAPAN, Achan 0/0/4/4 $48.00
PAPAW, Louis (Little) 0/0/2/2 $24.00
PAPAW, Louis 0/0/3/3 $36.00
PARKS, John 1/0/0/1 $12.00
PAS-KAH-ME 0/1/4/5 $60.00
PASH-CUM-GO-QUA 0/0/2/2 $24.00
PASH-ON 1/0/0/1 $12.00
PAW-BIT-TO 1/1/0/2 $24.00
PAW-HO-GO 1/1/4/6 $72.00
PAW-MECK-MUCK 1/0/1/2 $24.00
PAW-NUK-NUK 1/0/1/2 $24.00

PAW-SCO-WAHS 1/1/1/3 $36.00
PAWNEE, Lewis 0/1/0/1 $12.00
PAX-KAH 0/0/2/2 $24.00
PCAN (Deafy) 1/0/0/1 $12.00
PE-CAM-ZE 0/0/1/1 $12.00
PE-QUAN-QUA 0/0/1/1 $12.00
PE-SHE-GE-WIN 1/1/6/8 $96.00
PE-WE-SE-QUA 0/2/1/3 $36.00
PEAN 1/0/0/1 $12.00
PEAN-AH-GOT 0/0/1/1 $12.00
PEARSON, Mary 0/0/2/2 $24.00
PEARSON, John 1/0/0/1 $12.00
PEAT-WAT-MO-QUA 0/1/2/3 $36.00
PELTIER, Alex. 0/0/4/4 $48.00
PELTIER, Alex. Jr. 0/0/1/1 $12.00
PELTIFER, Geo. 0/1/4/5 $60.00
PEM-BO-GO 0/0/4/4 $48.00
PERU-MO 0/0/4/4 $48.00
PHELPS, Peter 0/0/2/2 $24.00
PHELPS, Wm. 0/0/4/4 $48.00
PI-O 0/0/2/2 $24.00
PIERCE, C. T. 1/0/0/1 $12.00
PKIH-SHE 0/1/1/2 $24.00
PNAS-SE-QUA 0/1/2/3 $36.00
POKE-TE-GO-QUA 0/0/1/1 $12.00
POLK, James K. 1/1/1/3 $36.00
PTES-SAH 0/0/2/2 $24.00
PUA-SWA-MDE-ME-KA 0/0/3/3 $36.00
PUK-IES 0/0/1/1 $12.00
PUK-KIS 1/1/4/6 $72.00
PUK-SUM 1/1/1/3 $36.00
QUA-O-DIP (?) 0/1/2/3 $36.00
QUA-WISH 0/1/2/3 $36.00
QUA-ZAS 0/1/0/1 $12.00
QUAH-QUAP 1/1/3/5 $60.00
QUAK-KAHB-WE 1/0/0/1 $12.00
RHODD, Fanny 0/0/5/5 $60.00
RHODD, David 0/1/2/3 $36.00
RICE, Mrs. 0/2/3/5 $60.00
RICE, Jack 1/0/0/1 $12.00
ROBINSON, Wm. 0/0/1/1 $12.00
SA-GAH-KNUK 0/0/3/3 $36.00
SACTO, Francis 1/0/1/2 $24.00
SAGE, Aaron 0/0/2/2 $24.00
SAH-GAH-CO-NUCK (Old) 0/0/1/1 $12.00
SAH-SAH-TON-GAH 0/0/2/2 $24.00
SAHG-MAG 0/0/1/1 $12.00
SAHG-NOSH-QUA 0/0/2/2 $24.00
SAHW-WE 0/1/1/2 $24.00
SAMS, Angeline 0/0/1/1 $12.00

SCROGGINS, Ellen 0/0/3/3 $36.00
SE-PI-O 1/1/2/4 $48.00
SHAB-NE 1/0/0/1 $12.00
SHAH-BWA-DUK 0/0/3/3 $36.00
SHAHN-NUH-NO-QUA 0/2/2/4 $48.00
SHE-GNA-GE 1/0/0/1 $12.00
SHEP-BE 1/1/3/5 $60.00
SHI-OCK-BE 1/0/0/1 $12.00
SHIM-NON-COTE 1/1/0/2 $24.00
SHIP-SHE 1/0/0/1 $12.00
SHIP-SHE-WAH-NO 0/1/4/5 $60.00
SHIS-KO 1/1/2/4 $48.00
SHKA-ZAH 1/1/3/5 $60.00
SHKEN-WA 1/1/4/6 $72.00
SHKIT-TO 1/1/3/5 $60.00
SHMAH-GAH 0/1/0/1 $12.00
SHOEN-MAH 0/0/2/2 $24.00
SHOLE-WA-TUK 1/1/0/2 $24.00
SHOLE-WY-TUCK 1/0/0/1 $12.00
SHOP-TESE-PAM-BO-GO 0/0/1/1 $12.00
SHOW-NA-SEE 1/2/6/9 $108.00
SHOW-NEH-GAH-BWE 1/0/2/3 $36.00
SHOW-NOSH 1/0/4/5 $60.00
SHOW-NUM-DA 0/1/3/4 $48.00
SHOW-WE 0/0/4/4 $48.00
SHOWE, Mary 0/1/0/1 $12.00
SIG-NAHK 1/2/4/7 $84.00
SIG-NAUH 0/0/1/1 $12.00
SIOUX, Alex 0/0/2/2 $24.00
SIS-BE-GEN 0/1/0/1 $12.00
SKE-MA 1/0/0/1 $12.00
SLAVEN, Tom 0/0/1/1 $12.00
SLAVEN, James 0/0/2/2 $24.00
SMITH, S. W. 1/0/4/5 $60.00
SMITH, Andy 0/0/3/3 $36.00
SMITH, Henry 0/0/1/1 $12.00
SMITH, Andy 0/0/1/1 $12.00
SOG-GHE-QUA 0/2/0/2 $24.00
SOG-MUK-SHUK 1/0/0/1 $12.00
SOLDIER, John 0/1/0/1 $12.00
SOUCIE, Peter 1/1/1/3 $36.00
SPENCER 1/0/0/1 $12.00
SUP-PA 0/1/1/2 $24.00
TAH-BAHS 0/1/0/1 $12.00
TAH-TAH-WEN 0/1/1/2 $24.00
TE-QUAH-KET 0/0/3/3 $36.00
TECIE, Antoine 0/0/6/6 $72.00
THOMPSON, Wm. 0/0/2/2 $24.00
THOMPSON, J. C. 0/0/2/2 $24.00
THOMPSON, James 1/0/0/1 $12.00

THURBUR, Ben 0/0/2/2 $24.00
TOM-MA, Rich'd 0/0/1/1 $12.00
TOMMA 1/0/0/1 $12.00
TRAVIS, A. E. 0/0/4/4 $48.00
TREMBLE, Louis 0/0/2/2 $24.00
TRUCKEY, Joseph 0/2/0/2 $24.00
TUCK-MEN, Paul 1/1/0/2 $24.00
VAN ARSDALE, G. B. 0/0/3/3 $36.00
VESSEUR, Susan 0/0/2/2 $24.00
VIEUX, Charles 0/0/4/4 $48.00
VIEUX, Ellen 0/1/0/1 $12.00
VIEUX, Louis Jr. 0/0/1/1 $12.00
VIEUX, Narcise 0/0/3/3 $36.00
VIEUX, Jacob 0/0/4/4 $48.00
VIEW, Charlotte 0/0/1/1 $12.00
WA-BEN-SEH 0/0/2/2 $24.00
WA-DO-DA-WAH 1/0/0/1 $12.00
WA-GESH-GO-MID 1/0/2/3 $36.00
WA-GO-SA 1/0/0/1 $12.00
WA-ME-GO 1/1/3/5 $60.00
WA-ME-GO 1/1/0/2 $24.00
WA-SAH-CO-UK 1/1/3/5 $60.00
WA-SHA 0/1/2/3 $36.00
WAB-NUM 0/1/2/3 $36.00
WAH-KAS, Archange 0/1/1/2 $24.00
WAH-KAS 1/0/1/2 $24.00
WAH-MAHS-MO-QUA (Wa-gesh-go) 0/1/0/1 $12.00
WAH-SA-SHKUK 1/0/0/1 $12.00
WAH-SAH-TO 0/0/1/1 $12.00
WAH-WAH-SOCK 1/0/0/1 $12.00
WAH-WAHG-BO 1/1/3/5 $60.00
WAH-WAHK-QUA 0/1/4/5 $60.00
WAH-WAHS-MO-QUA (Kah-kas) 0/1/0/1 $12.00
WAH-WAHS-MO-QUA (Crossed off on list)
WAH-WID-MO-QUA 0/0/2/2 $24.00
WAHB-KAH-BAH 2/1/3/6 $72.00
WAHB-PE-SHE 0/1/2/3 $36.00
WAHB-QUE 1/0/0/1 $12.00
WAHB-SACH 2/0/0/2 $24.00
WAHB-SHKIN 1/1/1/3 $36.00
WAHB-SKE 1/1/4/6 $72.00
WAHB-SOSE 1/0/0/1 $12.00
WAHB-SUM-QUA 0/1/0/1 $12.00
WAHLE-ZEA-SHKUK 1/0/0/1 $12.00
WAHS-NUG-GWA 0/0/2/2 $24.00
WAIN-MAG 1/1/1/3 $36.00
WAJ-GE-DA 1/1/4/6 $72.00
WAN-DAH-GA 1/0/1/2 $24.00
WE-QUAHS 1/1/0/2 $24.00
WE-WE-SAY 0/0/3/3 $36.00

WE-WE-SAY, Wm. 0/0/1/1 $12.00
WE-ZO 1/0/0/1 $12.00
WE-ZO-ZO-ZA 1/1/0/2 $24.00
WEAN-BE-A-GO 0/0/1/1 $12.00
WEH-WAHS-MO-QUA (Sepeo) 0/1/0/1 $12.00
WEK-JA 1/0/0/1 $12.00
WELCH, Joseph 0/0/2/2 $24.00
WELD, W. H. 0/0/3/3 $36.00
WELDFELT, Joseph 0/1/5/6 $72.00
WEMP-TE-GO-SHESE 0/0/3/3 $36.00
WEN-BE-TUCK 1/1/3/5 $60.00
WEW-TU-CO-SHE-QUA 0/1/2/3 $36.00
WHITE THUNDER 1/2/6/9 $108.00
WHITE 1/1/5/7 $84.00
WHITEHEAD, John 1/0/0/1 $12.00
WICKENS, V. 0/0/2/2 $24.00
WILMETTE, Louis 0/0/2/2 $24.00
WILMETTE, Joseph 0/0/6/6 $72.00
WILMETTE, Mrs. E. 0/0/2/2 $24.00
WILMETTE, Louis 0/0/4/4 $48.00
WILSON, John 0/0/1/1 $12.00
WIS-KA 1/0/0/1 $12.00
WISH-KO-BE-WA 0/0/2/2 $24.00
WISH-KUH-CASH-KUK 1/1/1/3 $36.00
WISH-TE-AH 1/0/1/2 $24.00
YAH-BA 1/0/3/4 $48.00
YATT, Louisa 0/0/1/1 $12.00
YATT, James 0/0/4/4 $48.00
YOUNG, G. L. 0/0/3/3 $36.00
ZE-BE-QUA 0/1/3/4 $48.00
ZE-ZE-TA 1/0/0/1 $12.00
ZHA-QUA-NAH 1/1/3/5 $60.00
ZHA-ZAH-NO 0/0/1/1 $12.00
ZHA-ZAHK-BE 1/0/0/1 $12.00
ZHAH-BWA-ZAH 1/0/0/1 $12.00
ZO-ZAS (American) 1/0/0/1 $12.00
ZO-ZAS 0/1/1/2 $24.00
ZO-ZAS (Sac) 1/0/0/1 $12.00
ZO-ZAS-MSHAH-BO 0/0/4/4 $48.00

1874 ANNUITY ROLL FOR YEAR
POTAWATOMI OF HURON

PAMP TWAY PE, Phineas Chief 1/1/4/6 $39.00 #1
ME ME 1/1/7/9 $58.50 #2
PAMP TWAY PE, John 1/1/5/7 $45.50 #3
KEY TOSH 1/1/5/7 $45.50 #4
MACKIE 1/1/4/6 $39.00 #5
MAW DO KAY 1/1/3/5 $32.50 #6

49

WAY ME NAW WAN 1/1/1/3 $19.50 #7
E DO WE KE ZHICK 1/1/1/3 $19.50 #8
WE ZO 1/0/1/2 $13.00 #9
WATSON, Amos 1/0/0/1 $6.50 #10
MAW KAW DAY O SIN 1/0/0/1 $6.50 #11
MACKIE, Mary 0/1/0/1 $6.50 #12
KAW BAISH KAW NO QUAY 0/1/0/1 $6.50 #13
AW GE MAW 0/1/0/1 $6.50 #14
DAVID, Silas 1/1/0/2 $13.00 #15
MAW GO QUAY 2/1/0/3 $19.50 #16
NO WAY SAY 1/1/1/3 $19.50 #17

<hr>

1875 ANNUITY ROLL FOR YEAR
POTAWATOMI OF HURON

PAMP TWAY PE, Phineas Chief 1/1/4/6 $39.00 #1
ME ME 1/1/7/9 $58.50 #2
PAMP TWAY PE, John 1/1/6/8 $52.00 #3
KEY TOSH 1/1/6/8 $52.00 #4
MACKIE 1/1/4/6 $39.00 #5
MON DO KAY 1/1/3/5 $32.50 #6
WAY ME NAW NAN 1/1/1/3 $19.50 #7
E DO WE KE ZHICK 1/1/1/3 $19.50 #8
WE ZO 1/0/1/2 $13.00 #9
WATSON, James 1/0/0/1 $6.50 #10
MAW KAW DAY O SIN 1/0/0/1 $6.50 #11
MACKIE, Mary 0/1/0/1 $6.50 #12
KAW BUSH KAW NO QUAY 1/0/0/1 $6.50 #13
DAVID, Silas 1/0/0/1 $6.50 #14
MAIR GO QUAY 1/2/1/4 $26.00 #15
NO WAY SAY 1/1/0/2 $13.00 #16

<hr>

1876 ANNUITY ROLL FOR YEAR
POTAWATOMI OF HURON

PAMP TWAY PE, Phineas Chief 1/1/5/7 $50.00 #1 Rem:
          Phineas Pamp te pe
ME MEE 1/1/8/10 $71.43 #2
PAMP TWAY PE, John 1/1/6/8 $57.13 #3
KEY TOSH 1/0/5/6 $42.86 #4 Rem: St. Jo. Co.
MACKIE 1/1/4/6 $42.86 #5
MON DO KAY 1/1/4/6 $42.86 #6
WAY MA WAH MAN 1/1/1/3 $21.43 #7
E DO WE KE ZHICK 1/1/1/3 $21.43 #8
WE ZO #9 Rem: Allegan; gone 4 years
WATSON, James #10 Rem: Indiana; no claim wife & two
          children Chippewa; gone

MAW CAU DOY O SIN #11 Rem: gone to Canada; left the
        tribe, married a white woman
MACKIE, Mary 0/1/0/1 $7.14 #12
KAW BUSH KAW NO QUAY 0/1/0/1 $7.14 #13
DAVID, Silas 1/0/0/1 $7.14 #14 Rem: hunting
MAIR GO QUAY 1/1/2/4 $28.58 #15
NO WAY SAY #16 Rem: dead

1877 ANNUITY ROLL FOR YEAR
POTAWATOMI OF HURON

PAMP TAYPEE, Phineas (Chief) 45 m $43.56 #1
        Mary wife 37 f #2
        Rodney son 18 m #3
        Frank son 12 m #4
        Jacob son 6 m #5
        George son 3 m #6
        Stephen son 1 m #7
ME MEE 48 m $62.23 #8
        Elizabeth wife 46 f #9
        Mary dau 24 f #10
        Jane dau 21 f #11
        Mary Ann dau 18 f #12
        Martha dau 16 f #13
        Joseph son 14 m #14
        Angeline dau 6 f #15
        Marchee (or Marcia) dau 3 f #16
        Lucy dau 2 f #17
PAMP TAY PE, John 52 m $49.79 #18
        Mary wife 35 f #19
        Makie (or Henry) son 20 m #20
        John son 19 m #21
        George son 17 m #22
        Frank son 13 m #23
        Samuel son 6 m #24
        Warren son 2 m #25
KEY TOSH 48 m $37.34 #26 Rem: wife white
        Basll son 16 m #27
        Chauncey son 14 m #28
        Henry son 12 m #29
        Samuel son 7 m #30
        Caroline dau 2 f #31
MAKIE 59 m $37.36 #32
        Nancy wife 50 f #33
        Anna dau 20 f #34
        John son 14 m #35
        Augustus son 12 m #36
        Thomas son 7 m #37

51

MON DO KAY 65 m $31.13 #38
        Charlotte wife 46 f #39
        Joseph son 19 m #40
        Samuel son 13 m #41
        Daniel son 4 m #42
WAY NA WAH 30 m $18.67 #43
        Josephine wife 25 f #44
        John son 3 m #45
E DO WE KE ZHICK 63 m $18.67 #46
        Nancy wife 45 f #47
        Isaac son 5 m #48
MAKIE, Mary 30 f $6.22 #49
KAW BASH KAW MO QUAY 35 f $6.22 #50
DAVID, Silas #--
MAIR GO QUAY 27 $18.63 #51
        Jacob bro 17 #52
        Lucy sis 16 #53
WEZOO, Thomas 37 m $31.12 #54 Rem: wife not a member
            of this tribe; Rec'd $26.22 on account of
            last years payment self & 3 children
        Addie Bell dau 8 f #55
        Eunice dau 4 f #56
        Dewitt son 2 m #57
        Mary dau 8mo f #58
WATSON, James 30 m $6.22 #59 Rem: or Amos as he is
            sometimes called; Wife Chippewa, not member
            of tribe, absent 4 years, no children known;
            this amount $6.56 due from last years
            payment

Silas David and Mair-co-day-o-sin are not entitled to
money or payment. David being a Chippewa of Saginaw,
Swan Creek & Black River, Mair-co-day-o-sin has gone
to Canada, married a white woman and abandoned all
tribal relations and intercourse. I have dropped their
names from the roll at the request of the members of
the tribe, as they were only allowed to have their
names upon the list, because they came here, and
lived, and permitted to share in former payments on
that account. Mair-co-doy-o-sin is supposed to have
gone back to Canada.

_____

1878 ANNUITY ROLL FOR YEAR
POTAWATOMI OF HURON

PAMPTEPE, Phineas (Chief) 45 m $43.75 #1
        Mary wife 38 f #2
        Rodney son 19 m #3
        Frank son 13 m #4

```
          Jacob son 7 m #5
          George son 4 m #6
          Stephen son 2 m #7
ME ME 49 m $62.50 #8
          Elizabeth wife 47 f #9
          Mary dau 24 f #10
          Jane dau 22 f #11
          Mary Ann dau 19 f #12
          Martha (or Marcia) dau 17 f #13
          Joseph son 15 m #14
          Angeline dau 7 f #15
          Marchee dau 4 f #16
          Lucy dau 3 f #17
PAMP TE PE, John 53 m $56.25 #18
          Mary wife 35 f #19
          Makie (or Henry) son 21 m #20
          John son 20 m #21
          George son 18 m #22
          Frank son 14 m #23
          Samuel son 7 m #24
          Warren son 3 m #25
          Addie dau 5mo f #26
KEY TOSH 49 m $37.50 #27
          Buel son 17 m #28
          Chauncey son 15 m #29
          Henry son 13 m #30
          Samuel son 8 m #31
          Caroline dau 3 f #32
SAU GAW QUE, Makie 53 m $31.25 #33
          Nancy wife 51 f #34
          John son 15 m #35
          Augustus son 13 m #36
          Thomas son 8 m #37
MON DO KAY 66 m $31.25 #38
          Charlotte wife 47 f #39
          Joseph son 20 m #40
          Samuel son 14 m #41
          Daniel son 5 m #42
WAY NA WAH 31 m $18.75 #43
          Josephine wife 26 f #44
          John son 4 m #45
E DO WE KE ZHICK 64 m $18.67 #46
          Nancy wife 46 f #47
          Isaac son 6 m #48
MAKIE, Mary 31 f $6.25 #49
KAW BASH KAW MO QUAY 36 f $6.25 #50
MAIR GO QUAY 28 f $18.75 #51
          Jacob bro 18 #52
          Lucy sis 17 #53
```

WEZOO, Thomas 38 m $37.50 #54
    Addie dau 9 f #55
    Eunice dau 5 f #56
    Dewitt son 3 m #57
    Mary dau 1 f #58
    Rosa wife 21 f #59
PO-KA-GON, Anna 21 f $12.50 #60 Rem: dau of #33
    Che-gar dau 2mo f #61
WATSON, Amos (or James) 32 m $18.75 #62
    Elizabeth wife 34 f #63
    Mary dau 1 f #64

1879 ANNUITY ROLL FOR YEAR
POTAWATOMI OF HURON

PAMPTEPE, Phineas (Chief) 46 m $40.58 #1
    Mary wife 39 f #2
    Rodney son 20 m #3
    Frank son 14 m #4
    Jacob son 10 m #5
    George son 5 m #6
    Stephen son 3 m #7
ME ME 50 m $63.77 #8
    Elizabeth wife 48 f #9
    Mary dau 25 f #10
    Jane dau 23 f #11
    Martha (or Marcia) dau 18 f #12
    Joseph son 16 m #13
    Angeline dau 8 f #14
    Marchee dau 5 f #15
    Lucy dau 4 f #16
    Mary Ann dau 20 f #17
    Shi-anno gson 2mo m #18 Rem: son of Mary Ann
PAMPTEPE, John 54 m $52.17 #19
    Mary wife 36 f #20
    Makie (or Henry) son 22 m #21
    John son 21 m #22
    George son 19 m #23
    Frank son 15 m #24
    Samuel son 8 m #25
    Warren son 4 m #26
    Addie dau 1 f #27
KEY TOSH 50 m $34.78 #28
    Buel son 18 m #29
    Chauncey son 16 m #30
    Henry son 11 m #31
    Samuel son 9 m #32
    Caroline dau 5 f #33

54

SAU GAW QUE, Makie 53 m $28.99 #34
    Nancy wife 52 f #35
    John son 16 m #36
    Augustus son 14 m #37
    Thomas son 9 m #38
MON-DO-QUE, Joseph 67 m $40.58 #39
    Charlotte wife 48 f #40
    Joseph Jr. son 21 m #41
    Samuel son 15 m #42
    Daniel son 6 m #43
    John gson 8mo m #44 Rem: son of Joseph Jr.
    Angeline dau-in-law 20 f #45 Rem: wife of Joseph
        Jr.
WAY NA WAH 32 m $23.19 #46
    Josephine wife 27 f #47
    John son 5 m #48
    Peter son 2mo m #49
EDO WE GE ZHICK 65 m $17.39 #50
    Nancy wife 47 f #51
    Isaac son 7 m #52
MAKIE, Mary 32 f $5.80 #53
KAW BASH KAW MO GAY 37 f $5.80 #54
MAUN GO QUAY 29 f $23.19 #55
    Frederick son 1mo m #56
    Jacob bro 19 #57
    Lucy sis 18 #58
WEZOO, Thomas 39 m $40.58 #59
    Rosa wife 22 f #60
    Addie dau 10 f #61
    Eunice dau 6 f #62
    Dewitt son 4 m #63
    Mary dau 2 f #64
    Martha dau 5mo f #65
PO-KA-GON, Anna 22 f $11.59 #66
    Che-gee dau 1 f #67
WATSON, Amos 33 m $11.59 #68 Rem: money unpaid 1876 &
        1877 $12.78
    Elizabeth wife 35 f #69

1880 ANNUITY ROLL FOR YEAR
POTAWATOMI OF HURON

PAMPTEPE, Phineas (Chief) 47 m $46.67 #1
    Mary wife 40 f #2
    Rodney son 21 m #3
    Frank son 15 m #4
    Jacob son 11 m #5
    George son 6 m #6
    Stephen son 4 m #7

ME MEE 51 m $60.00 #8
    Elizabeth wife 49 f #9
    Mary dau 26 f #10
    Jane dau 24 f #11
    Martha (or Marcia) dau 19 f #12
    Joseph son 17 m #13
    Angeline dau 9 f #14
    Marchee gdau 6 f #15
    Lucy dau 5 f #16
PAMPTEPE, John 55 m $60.01 #17
    Mary wife 37 f #18
    Markie (or Harry) son 23 m #19
    John son 22 m #20
    George son 20 m #21
    Frank son 16 m #22
    Samuel son 9 m #23
    Warren son 5 m #24
    Addie gdau 1 f #25
KEY TOSH 51 m Rem: not allow to participate as the
           family was never a member of this tribe
           having come from Tippecanoe, Indiana and
           allowed to be paid by a former chief who is
           now dead
    Buel son 19 m
    Chauncey son 17 m
    Henry son 12 m
    Samuel son 10 m
    Caroline dau 6 f
SAW GAU QUE, Makie 54 m $33.33 #26
    Nancy wife 53 f #27
    John son 17 m #28
    Augustus son 15 m #29
    Thomas son 10 m #30
MAUN DO KAY, Joseph 68 m $26.66 #31
    Charlotte wife 49 f #32
    Samuel son 16 m #33
    Daniel son 7 m #34
MAUN DO KAY, Joseph Jr. 22 m $26.68 #35 Rem: son of
         #31
    Angeline wife 21 f #36
    John son 1 m #37
    William son 1mo m #38
WAY NA WAH 33 m $26.66 #39
    Josephine wife 28 f #40
    John son 6 m #41
    Peter son 1 m #42
EDO WE GE ZHICK 66 m $20.00 #43
    Nancy wife 48 f #44
    Isaac son 8 m #45
MAKIE, Mary 33 f $6.66 #46

KAW KAW MO QUAY 38 f Rem: member of Chippewa Tribe of
        Indians of Saginaw, Swan Creek & Black
        River, heretofore allowed by tribe to
        participate in payments of this tribe, but
        now not with standing still lives in the
        neighborhood but was objected to.
MAUN GO QUAY 30 f Rem: members of Chippewa Tribe of
        Indians of Saginaw, Swan Creek & Black
        River, heretofore allowed by tribe to
        participate in payments of this tribe, but
        now not with standing still lives in the
        neighborhood, but was objected to.
    Jacob bro 20
    Nancy sis 18
    Frederick son 1 m
WE ZOO, Thomas 40 m $46.72 #47
    Rosa wife 22 f #48
    Addie dau 11 f #49
    Eunice dau 7 f #50
    Dewitt son 5 m #51
    Mary dau 3 f #52
    Martha dau 1 f #53
POKAGON, Anna 23 f $13.34 #54
    Che Ge dau 2 f #55
WATSON, Amos 34 m $20.00 #56
    Elizabeth wife 35 f #57
    Etta Alice dau 9mo f #58
WEZOO, Mary Ann 21 f $13.32 #59 Rem: dau of #8
    Frederick son 1 m #60

1882 ANNUITY ROLL FOR YEAR
POTAWATOMI OF HURON

PAMPTEPE, Phineas (Chief) 48 m $37.33 #1
    Mary wife 41 f #2
    Rodney son 22 m #3
    Frank son 16 m #4
    Jacob son 12 m #5
    George son 7 m #6
    Stephen son 5 m #7
ME MEE 52 m $48.00 #8
    Elizabeth wife 50 f #9
    Mary dau 27 f #10
    Jane dau 25 f #11
    Martha (or Marcia) dau 20 f #12
    Joseph son 18 m #13
    Angeline dau 10 f #14
    Marchee gdau 7 f #15
    Lucy dau 6 f #16

57

PAMPTEPE, John 56 m $48.00 #17
        Mary wife 38 f #18
        Markie (or Harry) son 24 m #19
        John Jr. son 23 m #20
        George son 21 m #21
        Frank son 17 m #22
        Samuel son 10 m #23
        Warren son 6 m #24
        Addie gdau 2 f #25
KEY TOSH 52 m $32.00 #26
        Buel son 20 m #27
        Chauncy son 17 m #28
        Henry son 13 m #29
        Samuel son 11 m #30
        Caroline dau 7 f #31
SAW GAU QUE, Makie 55 m $26.67 #32
        Nancy wife 54 f #33
        John son 18 m #34
        Augustus son 16 m #35
        Thomas son 11 m #36
MAUN DO KAY, Joseph 69 m $21.33 #37
        Charlotte wife 50 f #38
        Samuel son 17 m #39
        Daniel son 8 m #40
MAUN DO KAY, Joseph Jr. 23 m $21.33 #41 Rem: son of
        #37
        Angeline wife 21 f #42
        John son 1 m #43
        William son 1mo m #44
WAY NA WAH 34 m $21.33 #45
        Josephine wife 29 f #46
        John son 7 m #47
        Peter son 2 m #48
EDO WE GE ZHICK 67 m $16.00 #49
        Nancy wife 49 f #50
        Isaac son 9 m #51
NAW NAW QUE BE 28 m $32.10 #52
        Maun go quay wife 31 f #53
        Jacob bro-in-law 21 #54
        Nancy sis-in-law 19 #55
        Frederick son 2 m #56 Rem: son Maun go qua
        Elizabeth dau 1 f #57
WE ZOO, Thomas 41 m $42.86 #58
        Rosa wife 23 f #59
        Addie dau 12 f #60
        Eunice dau 8 f #61
        Dewitt son 6 m #62
        Mary dau 4 f #63
        Martha dau 2 f #64
        Agnes dau 8mo f #65

PO KA GON, Anna 24 f $5.33 #66
    Che Ge dau 3 f
WATSON, Amos 35 m $20.00 #67
    Elizabeth wife 36 f #68
    Etta Alice dau 1 f #69
WEZOO, Mary Ann 22 f $16.00 #70 Rem: dau of #8
    Frederick son 2 m #71
    Martha dau 10mo f #72
AISH CO BAY 55 m $5.33 #73
NUM QUA TO WE 34 m $10.70 #74
    Mary wife 34 f #75

————————

1883 ANNUITY ROLL FOR YEAR
POTAWATOMI OF HURON

PAMP-TE-PE, Phineas (Chief) 49 m $37.33 #1
    Mary wife 42 f #2
    Frank son 17 m #3
    Jacob son 13 m #4
    George son 8 m #5
    Stephen son 6 m #6
PAMP-TE-PE, Rodney 23 m $5.19 #7 Rem: son of #1 live
    now by himself
ME-MEE (Raisen Sap) 53 m $46.80 #8
    Elizabeth wife 51 f #9
    Mary dau 28 f #10
    Martha (or Marcia) dau 21 f #11
    Joseph son 19 m #12
    Angeline dau 19 f #13
    Marchee gdau 8 f #14
    Lucy dau 7 f #15
    Louis son 6mo m #16
PAMP-TE-PE, John 57 m $41.60 #17
    Mary wife 39 f #18
    Mackie (or Harry) son 25 m #19
    George son 22 m #20
    Frank son 18 m #21
    Samuel son 11 m #22
    Warren son 7 m #23
    Addie gdau 3 f #24
PAMP-TE-PE, John Jr. 23 m $20.76 #25
    Jane wife 26 f #26
    Susan sdau 8 f #27 Rem: dau of Jane
    Mary dau 1 f #28
KE-TOSH 53 m $31.20 #29
    Buel son 21 m #30
    Chauncy son 19 m #31
    Henry son 14 m #32
    Samuel son 12 m #33

```
          Caroline dau 8 f #34
SAW-QAW-QUE, Mackie 56 m $25.95 #35
     Nancy wife 55 f #36
     John son 19 m #37
     Augustus son 16 m #38
     Thomas son 12 m #39
MAUN-DO-KAY, Joseph 70 m $20.80 #40
     Charlotte wife 51 f #41
     Samuel son 18 m #42
     Daniel son 9 m #43
MAUN-DO-KAY, Joseph Jr. 24 m $20.76 #44 Rem: son of
          #40
     Angeline wife 23 f #45
     John son 3 m #46
     Elizabeth dau 6mo m #47 Rem: died Feb 1883 age 6
          months
WAY NA WEH 35 m $20.80 #48
     Josephine wife 30 f #49
     John son 8 m #50
     Peter son 3 m #51
E-DO-WE-GE-ZHICK 68 m $15.57 #52
     Nancy wife 50 f #53
     Isaac son 10 m #54
NAW-NAW-QUA-BE (Stephen Mackie) 29 m $31.20 #55
     Maun-go-quoy wife 32 f #56
     Frederick son 3 m #57
     Elizabeth dau 2 f #58
     Jacob bro-in-law 21 #59 Rem: bro of #56
     Nancy sis-in-law 19 #60 Rem: sis of #56
POKAGON, Anna 25 f $10.38 #61
     Infant (unnamed) son 4wk #62
WE ZOO, Thomas 42 m $31.14 #63
     Rosa wife 24 f #64
     Addie dau 13 f #65
     Eunice dau 9 f #66
     Mary dau 5 f #67
     Agnes dau 18mo f #68
WE ZOO, Mary Ann 23 f $15.57 #69
     Frederic son 3 m #70
     Martha dau 2 f #71
NUM-QUA-TO-WAH 35 m $10.38 #72
     Mary wife 35 f #73
WATSON, Amos 36 m $20.76 #74
     Elizabeth wife 37 f #75
     Etta Alice dau 2 f #76
     John son 4mo m #77
```

PAMP-TE-PE, Phineas Chief 50 m 1/1 $31.20
    Mary wife 48 f 2/2
    Frank son 18 m 3/3
    Jacob son 14 m 4/4
    George son 9 m 5/5
    Stephen son 1 m 6/6
PAMP-TE-PE, Rodney 24 m 7/7 $5.20
ME-MEE (Raisen Sap) 54 m 8/8 $31.20
    Elizabeth wife 52 f 9/9
    Mary dau 29 f 10/10 $5.20
    Martha dau 22 f 11/11 $5.20
    Angeline dau 20 f 13/12
    Lucy dau 8 f 15/13
    Joseph son 20 m 12/14
    Louis son 2 m 16/15
PAMP-TE-PE, John 58 m 17/16 $26.00
    Mary wife 40 f 18/17
    Mackie (or Harry) son 26 m 19/18 $5.20
    George son 23 m 20/19 $5.20
    Samuel son 12 m 22/20
    Warren son 8 m 23/22
    Addie dau 4 f 24/22 Rem: Incorrectly enrolled
        last year as their granddau
PAMP-TE-PE, John, Jr. 25 m 25/23 $20.80
    Jane wife 27 f 26/24
    Susan sdau 9 f 14&27/25 Rem: child of Jane
    Mary dau 2 f 28/26
KE-TOSH 54 m 29/27 $26.00
    Chauncey son 20 m 31/28
    Henry son 15 m 32/29
    Samuel son 13 m 33/30
    Caroline dau 9 f 34/31
SAW-GAW-QUE, Mackie 57 m 35/32 $20.80
    John son 20 m 37/33
    Augustus son 17 m 38/34
    Thomas son 13 m 39/35
MAUN-DO-KAY, Joseph 71 m 40/36 $20.78
    Charlotte wife 52 f 41/37
    Samuel son 19 m 42/38
    Daniel son 10 m 43/39
MAUN-DO-KA, Joseph, Jr. 25 m 44/40 $??.??
    Angeline wife f 45/41 Rem: died Apr 15, 1884
    John son 4 m 46/42
    Joseph son 2mo m -/43
WAY-NA-WEH 36 m 48/44 $25.95
    Josephine wife 31 f 49/45
    John son 9 m 50/46

```
              Peter son 4 m 51/47
              William son 10mo -/48
E-DO-WE-GE-ZHICK 69 m 52/49 $15.57
              Nancy wife 51 f 53/50
              Isaac son 11 m 54/51
NAW-NAW-QUA (Stephen Mackie) 30 m 55/52 $25.95
              Maun-go-quoi wife 33 f 56/53
              Frederick son 4 m 57/54
              Elizabeth dau 3 f 58/55
              Jeff son 5mo m -/56
NOON-WEH, Jacob 23 m 59/57 $5.19 Rem: bro of #56
              Lucy sis 21 f 60/58 $5.19 Rem: sis of #56; called
                  Nancy last year
POKAGON, Annie 26 f 61/59 $10.38
              Jennie dau 18mo f 61/60 Rem: unnamed last year
WE-ZOO, Thomas 43 m 63/61 $31.14
              Rosa wife 35 f 64/62
              Addie dau 14 f 65/63
              Eunice dau 10 f 66/64
              Mary dau 6 f 67/65
              Agnes dau 2 f 68/66
WE-ZOO, Mary Ann 24 f 69/67 $20.76
              Frederic son 4 m 70/68
              Martha dau 3 f 71/69
              Francis son 1 m -/70
NUM-QUA-TO-WAH (Wallace Hinman) 36 m 72/71 $10.38
              Mary wife 36 f 73/72
WATSON, Amos 37 m 74/73 $25.95
              Elizabeth wife 38 f 75/74
              Etta Alice dau 3 f 76/75
              John son 1 m 77/76 (died Aug 21, 1883)
              Maggie dau 1mo f -/77
```

1885 ANNUITY ROLL
POTAWATOMI OF HURON

```
PAMP-TE-PE, Phineas - Chief 51 m 1/1 $ 31.2?
              Mary wife 49 f 2/2
              Frank son 19 m 3/3
              Jacob son 15 m 4/4
              George son 10 m 5/5
              Stephen son 8 m 6/6
PAMP-TE-PE, Rodney 25 m 7/7 $5.20
ME-MEE (Raisen Sap) 55 m 8/8 $26.00
              Elizabeth wife 53 f 9/9
              Mary dau 30 f 10/10 $5.20
              Martha dau 23 f 11/11 $5.20
              Angeline dau 16 f 12/12 Rem: Her age by mistake
                  reported last year as 20; died Apr 16
```

Lucy dau 9 f 13/13
Joseph son 21 m 14/14 $5.20
Louis son 2 m 15/15 Rem: died Oct 27
PAMP-TE-PE, John 59 m 16/16 $??.??
    Mary wife 41 f 17/17
    Mackie (or Harry) son 27 m 18/18 $5.20
    George son 24 m 19/19 $5.20
    Samuel son 13 m 20/20
    Warren son 9 m 21/21
    Addie dau 5 f 22/22
PAMP-TE-PE, John, Jr. 26 m 23/23 $20.80
    Jane wife 28 f 24/24
    Susan sdau 10 f 25/25 Rem: dau of Jane
    Mary dau 3 f 26/26
KE-TOSH 55 m 27/27 $20.80
    Chauncey son 21 m 28/28 $5.20
    Henry son 16 m 29/29
    Samuel son 14 m 30/30
    Caroline dau 10 f 31/31
SAW-GAW-QUE, Mackie 58 m 32/32 $26.00
    John son 21 m 33/33 $5.20
    Augustus son 18 m 34/34
    Thomas son 14 m 35/35
POKAGON, Annie 26 f 59/36 Rem: dau of #32; died Dec
        13, 1884
    Jennie dau 2 f 60/37 Rem: lives with her
        grandfather #32 since her mother's death
MAUN-DO-KAY, Joseph 72 m 36/38 $25.95
    Charlotte wife 53 f 37/39
    Samuel son 20 m 38/40
    Jane dau-in-law 17 f ??/41 Rem: wife of Samuel;
        Ottawa married into Band, allowed on roll by
        vote of Band
    Daniel son 10 m 39/42 Rem: died Aug 20, 1884
MAUN-DO-KAY, Joseph, Jr. 26 m 40/43 $20.76
    Eliza wife 19 f ??/44 Rem: Ottawa married into
        Band allowed to draw by vote of Band
    John son 5 m 42/45
    Joseph son m 43/46
WAY-NA-WEH 37 m 44/47 $25.95
    Josephine wife 32 f 45/48
    John son 10 m 46/49
    Peter son 5 m 47/50
    William son m 48/51
E-DO-WE-GE-ZHICK 70 m 49/52 $15.57
    Nancy wife 52 f 50/53
    Isaac son 12 m 51/54
NAW-NAW-QUA-BE (Stephen Mackie) 31 m 52/55 $25.95
    Maun-go-quoi wife 34 f 53/56
    Frederick son 5 m 54/57

```
        Elizabeth dau 4 f 55/58
        Jeff son 1 m 56/59
NOON-WEH, Jacob 24 m 57/60 $5.19 Rem: bro of #56
        Lucy sis 22 f 58/61 $5.19 Rem: sis of #56
WE-ZOO, Thomas 44 m 61/62 $31.14
        Rosa wife 36 f 62/63
        Addie dau 15 f 63/64
        Eunice dau 11 f 64/65
        Mary dau 7 f 65/66
        Agnes dau 3 f 66/67
WE-ZOO, Mary Ann 25 f 67/68 $20.76
        Frederic 5 m 68/69
        Martha dau 4 f 69/70
        Francis son 2 m 70/71
NUM-QUA-TO-WAH (Wallace Hinman) 37 m 71/72 Rem: Not
            paid absent
        Mary wife 37 f 72/73 Rem: Not paid absent
WATSON, Amos 38 m 73/74 $20.76
        Elizabeth wife 39 f 74/75
        Etta Alice dau 7 f 75/76
        Maggie dau 9mo f 77/77 Rem: died Dec 3, 1884
```

1886 ANNUITY ROLL
POTAWATOMI OF HURON

```
PAMP-TE-PE, Phineas (Chief) 52 m 1/1 $30.42
        Mary wife 50 f 2/2
        Frank son 20 m 3/3
        Jacob son 16 m 4/4
        George son 11 m 5/5
        Stephen son 9 m 6/6
PAMP-TE-PE, Rodney 26 m 7/7 $5.07
ME-MEE (Raisin Sap) 56 m 8/8 $20.28
        Elizabeth wife 54 f 9/9
        Mary dau 31 f 10/10 Rem: died May 14, 1885
        Martha dau 24 f 11/11 $10.14
        Lucy dau 10 f 13/12 Rem: died May 9, 1885
        Joseph son 22 m 14/13 $5.07
        Atwood gson 4mo m -/14 Rem: son of Martha
PAMP-TE-PE, John 60 m 16/15 $25.35
        Mary wife 42 f 17/16
        Mackie (or Harry) son 28 m 18/17
        George son 25 m 19/18 $5.07
        Samuel son 14 m 20/19
        Warren son 10 m 21/20
        Addie dau 6 f 22/21 Rem: died May 4, 1885
PAMP-TE-PE, John, Jr. 27 m 23/22 $25.35
        Jane wife 28 f 24/23
```

Susan sdau 11 f 25/24 Rem: dau of Jane; died May
      9, 1885
   Mary dau 4 f 26/25
   Angeline dau 11mo -/26
KE-TOSH 56 m 27/27 $20.24
   Chauncey son 22 m 28/28 $5.06
   Henry son 17 m 29/29
   Samuel son 15 m 30/30
   Caroline dau 11 f 31/31
SAW-GAW-QUE, Mackie 59 m 32/32 $20.24
   John son 22 m 33/33 $5.06
   Augustus son 19 m 34/34
   Thomas son 15 m 35/35
POK-A-GON, Jennie 3 f 37/36 Rem: gdau of #32, dau of
      Annie Pok-a-gon the dau of #32
MAUN-DO-KAY, Joseph 73 m 38/37 $10.72
   Charlotte wife 54 f 39/38
   Samuel son 21 m 40/39
   Jane dau-in-law 18 f 41/40 Rem: wife of Samuel
   Daniel gson 4mo -/41 Rem: son of Samuel & Jane
MAUN-DO-KAY, Joseph, Jr. 27 m 43/42 $20.24
   Eliza wife 20 f 44/43
   John son 6 m 45/44
   Joseph son 2 m 46/45
WAY-NA-WEH 38 m 47/46 $30.36
   Josephine wife 33 f 48/47
   John son 11 m 49/48
   Peter son 6 m 50/49
   William son 3 m 51/50
   Frank son 1mo m -/51
E-DO-WE-GE-ZHICK 71 m 52/52 $15.18
   Nancy wife 53 f 53/53
   Isaac son 13 m 54/54
NAW-NAW-QUA-BE (Stephe Mackie) 32 m 55/55 $25.30
   Maun-go-quoi wife 33 f 56/56
   Fredrick son 6 m 57/57
   Elizabeth dau 5 f 58/58
   Jeff son 2 m 59/59
NOON-WEH, Jacob 25 m 60/60 $5.06 Rem: bro of #56
   Lucy sis 23 f 61/61 Rem: sis of #56
WE-ZOO, Thomas 45 m 62/62 $35.42
   Rosa wife 37 f 63/63
   Addie dau 16 f 64/64
   Mary dau 12 f 65/65
   Agnes dau 8 f 66/66
   Laura dau 1 f -/68
WE-ZOO, Mary Ann 26 f 68/69 $20.24
   Fredrick son 6 m 69/70
   Martha dau 5 f 70/71
   Francis son 3 m 71/72

NUM-QUA-TE-NAH (Wallace Hinman) 38 m 72/73 $10.12 Rem:
        was under arrest for violation of the law
        and could not be present
    Mary wife 38 f 73/74
WATSON, Amos 39 m 74/75 $20.24
    Elizabeth wife 40 f 75/76
    Etta Alice dau 5 76/77
    Nancy Jennie dau 6mo -/78
AISH-KE-BA, Francis m -/79

1887 ANNUITY ROLL
POTAWATOMI OF HURON

PAMPTE-PE, Phineas (Chief) 53 m 1/1 $26.30
    Mary wife 57 f 2/2
    Frank son 21 m 3/3 $5.26
    Jacob son 17 m 4/4
    George son 12 m 5/5
    Stephen son 10 m 6/6
PAMPTE-PE, Rodney 27 m 7/7 $5.26
MEE-NEE (Raisin Sap) 57 m 8/8 $10.52
    Elizabeth wife 55 f 9/9
    Martha dau 25 f 11/12 $10.52
    Joseph son 23 m 13/11 $5.26
    Atwood gson 5 m 14/12 Rem: son of Martha
PAMPTE-PE, John 61 m 15/13 $21.04
    Mary wife 43 f 16/14
    Mackie (or Hary) son 29 m 17/15 $5.26
    George son 26 m 18/16
    Samuel son 15 m 19/17
    Warren son 11 m 20/19
PAMPTE-PE, John Jr. 28 m 22/19 $21.04
    Jane wife 29 f 23/20
    Mary dau 5 f 25/21
    Angeline dau 2 f 26/22
KETOSH 57 m 27/23 $26.30
    Chaucy son 23 m 28/24
    Henry son 18 m 29/25
    Samuel son 16 m 30/26
    Caroline dau 12 f 31/27
SAW-GO-QUOT, Mackie 60 m 32/28 $21.04
    John son 23 m 33/29 $5.26
    Augustus son 20 m 34/30
    Thomas son 16 m 35/31
POK-A-GON, Jennie 5 f 36/32 Rem: gdau of #32, dau of
        Annie Pok-a-gon, who was a dau of #32
MANDOKAY, Joseph 74 m 37/33 $10.52
    Charlotte wife 55 f 38/34
    Samuel son 22 m 39/35 $16.78

66

Jane dau-in-law 19 f 40/36 Rem: wife of Samuel
David gson 16mo m 41/37 Rem: son of Samuel &
    Jane
MANDOKAY, Joseph Jr. 28 m 42/38 $26.30
    Eliza wife 21 f 43/39
    John son 7 m 44/40
    Joseph son 3 m 45/41
    Angeline dau 5mo f -/42
WAY-NA-WEH 39 m 46/43 $31.56
    Josephine wife 34 f 47/44
    John son 12 m 48/45
    Peter son 7 m 49/46
    William son 4 m 50/47
    Frank son 1 m 51/48
E-DO-WE-GE-ZHICK 72 m 52/49 $16.78
    Nancy wife 54 f 53/50
    Isaac son 14 m 54/51
NAW-NAW-QUABE (Stephen Mackie) 33 m 55/52 $26.34
    Maun-go-quoi wife 36 f 56/53
    Frederick son 7 m 57/54
    Elizabeth dau 6 f 58/55
    Jeff son 3 m 59/56
NOON-WEH, Jacob 26 m 60/57 $5.27 Rem: bro of #53
    Lucy sis 24 f 61/58 $5.27 Rem: sis of #53
WEE-ZOO, Thomas 46 m 62/59 $42.16
    Rosa wife 38 f 63/60
    Addie dau 17 f 64/61
    Eunice dau 13 f 65/62
    Mary dau 9 f 66/63
    Agnes dau 6 f 67/64
    Laura dau 2 f 68/65
    Nancy dau 1day f -/66
WEE-ZOO, Mary Ann 27 f 69/67 $21.08
    Frederick son 7 m 70/68
    Martha dau 6 f 71/69
    Francis son 4 m 72/70
MUN-QUA-TE-NAH (Wallace Hinman) 39 m 73/- Rem: not
        paid
    Mary wife 39 f 74/71 $5.27
WATSON, Amos 40 m 75/72 $21.08
    Elizabeth wife 41 f 76/73
    Etta Alice dau 6 f 77/74
    Nancy Jennie dau 18mo f 78/75
AISH-KE-BA, Francis 65 m 79/76 $5.27

———————

67

PAMPTE PE, Phineas (Chief) 54 m 1/1 $25.65
    Mary wife 52 f 2/2
    Frank son 22 m 3/3 $5.13
    Jacob son 18 m 4/4
    George son 13 m 5/5
    Stephen son 11 m 6/6
PAMPTE PE, Rodney 28 m 7/7 $5.13
MEE-NEE (Raisin Sap) 58 m 8/8 $10.26
    Elizabeth wife 56 f 9/9
    Martha dau 26 f 10/10 $15.39
    Joseph son 24 m 11/11 $5.13
    Attwood gson 6 m 12/12 Rem: son of Martha
    Lucy gdau 6mo f -/13 Rem: dau of Martha
PAMPTE PE, John 62 m 13/14 $20.52
    Mary wife 44 f 14/15
    Mackie or Harry son 36 m 15/16 $5.13
    George son 27 m 16/17 $5.13
    Samuel son 16 m 17/18
    Warren son 12 m 18/19
PAMPTE PE, John, Jr. 29 m 19/20 $20.52
    Jane wife 30 f 20/21
    Mary dau 6 f 21/22
    Angeline dau 22/23
KE-TOSH, Henry 19 m 25/24 $10.26
    Samuel bro 17 m 26/25
    Caroline sis 13 f 27/26 $5.13
SAW-GO-QUET, Mackie 61 m 28/27 $10.26
    John son 24 m 29/28 $5.13
    Augustus son 21 m 30/29 $5.13
    Thomas son 17 m 31/30
POKAGON, Jennie 6 f 32/31 $5.13 Rem: gdau of #27, dau
        of Annie Pokagon, dau of #27
MANDOKAY, Joseph 73 m 33/32 Rem: died Mar 18, 1888
    Charlotte wife 56 f 34/33 $10.26
    Samuel son 23 m 35/34 $15.39
    Jane dau-in-law 20 f 36/35 Rem: wife of Samuel
    Nancy gdau 2mo f -/36 Rem: dau of Samuel & Jane
MANDOKAY, Joseph, Jr. 29 m 38/37 $25.65
    Eliza wife 22 f 39/38
    John son 8 m 40/39
    Joseph son 41/40
    Angeline dau 1 f 42/41
WAY-NA-WEH 40 m 43/42 $35.91
    Josephine wife 35 f 44/43
    John son 13 m 45/44
    Peter son 8 m 46/45
    William son 5 m 47/46

Frank son 2 m 48/47 Rem: died Jul 30, 1887
      Phoeba dau 2mo f -/48
E-DO-WE-GE-ZHICK 73 m 49/49 $15.39
      Nancy wife 55 f 50/50
      Isaac son 15 m 51/51
NAW-NAW-QUABE (Stephen Mackie) 34 m 52/52 $20.52
      Maun-go-quoi wife 37 f 53/53
      Elizabeth dau 7 f 55/54
      Jeff son 4 m 56/55
NOON-WEH, Jacob 27 m 57/56 $5.13 Rem: bro of #53
      Lucy sis 25 f 58/57 $5.13 Rem: sis of #53
WEE-ZOO, Thomas 47 m 59/58 $41.03
      Rosa wife 39 f 60/59
      Addie dau 18 f 61/60
      Eunice dau 14 f 62/61
      Mary dau 10 f 63/62
      Agnes dau 7 f 64/63
      Laura dau 3 f 65/64 Rem: died Jul 28, 1887
      Nancy dau 1 f 66/65
WEE-ZOO, Mary Ann 28 f 67/66 $20.48
      Martha dau 7 f 69/67
      Francis son 5 m 70/68
      Peter son 7mo -/69
MUN-QUA-TE-NAH (Wallace Hinman) 40 m 70/-
      Mary wife 40 f 71/70 $5.12
WATSON, Amos 41 m 72/71 $25.60
      Elizabeth wife 42 f 73/72
      Etta Alice dau 8 f 74/73
      Nancy Jennie dau 3 f 75/74
      Sarah Ann dau 4mo f -/75
AISH-KE-BA, Francis 66 m 76/76
ISAAC, Sarah 44 f -/77 $10.24
      Nancy dau 11 f -/78

1889 ANNUITY ROLL FOR 1ST QTR
POTAWATOMI OF HURON

PAMPTE PE, Phineas Chief 55 m 1/1 $249.97
      Mary wife 53 f 2/2 $249.97
      Frank son 23 m 3/3 $249.97
      Jacob son 19 m 4/4 $249.97
      George son 14 m 5/5 $249.97
      Stephen son 12 m 6/6 $249.97
PAMPTE PE, Rodney 29 m 7/7 $249.97
MEE NEE (Raisin Sap) 59 m 8/8 $249.97
      Elizabeth wife 57 f 9/9 $249.97
      Joseph son 25 m 10/10 $249.97
ISAAC, Martha 27 f 11/11 $249.97 Rem: dau of #8 & #9
      Atwood son 7 m 12/12 $249.97

Lucy dau 1 f 13/13 $249.97 Rem: adopted by V. P.
    Isaac; dau of Martha
PAMPTE PE, John 63 m 14/14 $249.97
    Mary wife 45 f 15/15 $249.97
    Mackie or Harry son 31 m 16/16 $249.97
    George son 28 m 17/17 $249.97
    Samuel son 17 m 18/18 $249.97
    Warren son 13 m 19/19 $249.97
PAMPTE PE, John, Jr. 30 m 20/20 $249.97
    Jane wife 31 f 21/21 $249.97
    Mary dau 7 f 22/22 $249.97
    Angeline dau 4 f 23/23 $249.97
    Cyrus son 2wk m -/24 $249.97 Rem: not born when
    roll made
KETOSH, Henry 22 m 24/25 $249.97
    Samuel bro 18 m 25/26 $249.97
    Charlotte sis 14 f 26/27 $249.97
SAW-GO-QUOT, Mackie 62 m 27/28 $249.97
    John son 25 m 28/29 $249.97
    Augustus son 22 m 29/30 $249.97
    Thomas son 18 m 30/31 $249.97
POKAGON, Jennie 7 f 31/32 $250.55 Rem: gdau of #27
MANDOKAY, Charlotte 57 f 32/33 $249.97
MANDOKAY, Samuel 24 m 33/34 $249.97
    Jane wife 21 f 34/35 $249.97
    Nancy dau 1 f 35/36 $249.97
MANDOKAY, Joseph, Jr. 30 m 36/37 $249.67
    Eliza wife 23 f 37/38 $249.97
    John son 9 m 38/39 $249.97
    Joseph son 5 m 39/40 $249.97
    Angeline dau 2 f 40/41 $250.09
WAY-NA-WEH (David Notawa) 41 m 41/42 $249.97
    Josephine wife 36 f 42/43 $249.97
    John son 14 m 43/44 $249.97
    Peter son 9 m 44/45 $249.97
    William son 6 m 45/46 $249.97
    Phoeba dau 1 f 46/47 $249.97
E-DO-WE-GE-ZHICK 74 m 47/48 $249.97
    Nancy wife 56 f 48/49 $249.97
    Isaac son 16 m 49/50 $249.97
NAW-NAW-QUABE (Stephen Mackie) 35 m 50/51 $249.97
    Maun-go-quoi wife 38 f 51/52 $249.97
    Elizabeth dau 8 f 52/53 $249.97
    Jeff son 5 m 53/54 $249.97
NOON-WEH, Jacob 28 m 54/55 $249.97
    Lucy wife 26 f 55/56 $249.97
    Jacob, Jr. 1 m 56/57 $249.97
WEE-ZOO, Thomas 48 m 57/58 $249.97
    Rosa wife 40 f 58/59 $249.97
    Addie dau 19 f 59/60 $249.97

```
        Eunice dau 15 f 60/61 $249.97
        Mary dau 11 f 61/62 $249.97
        Agnes dau 8 f 62/63 $249.97
        Nancy dau 2 f 63/64 $249.97
WEE-ZOO, Mary Ann 29 f 64/65 $249.97
        Martha dau 8 f 65/66 $249.97
        Francis son 6 m 66/67 $249.97
        Peter son 1 m 67/68 $249.97
QUA-TE-NAH, Mary (Hinman) 41 f 68/69 $249.97
WATSON, Amos 42 m 69/70 $249.97
        Elizabeth wife 43 f 70/71 $249.97
        Etta Alice dau 9 f 71/72 $249.97
        Nancy Jennie dau 4 f 72/73 $249.97
        Sarah Ann dau 1 f 73/74 $249.97
ISAAC, Sarah 45 f 74/75 $249.97
        Nancy dau 12 f 75/76 $249.97
```

———————

1889 ANNUITY ROLL FOR YEAR
POTAWATOMI OF HURON

```
PAMPTE PE, Phineas Chief 55 m 1/1 $106.66
        Mary wife 53 f 2/2 $106.66
        Frank son 23 m 3/3 $106.66
        Jacob son 19 m 4/4 $106.66
        George son 14 m 5/5 $106.66
        Stephen son 12 m 6/6 $106.66
PAMPTE PE, Rodney 29 m 7/7 $106.66
MEE NEE (Raisin Sap) 59 m 8/8 $106.66
        Elizabeth wife 57 f 9/9 $106.66
        Joseph son 25 m 10/10 $106.66
ISAAC, Martha 27 f 11/11 $106.66 Rem: dau of #8 & #9
        Atwood son 7 m 12/12 $106.66
        Lucy dau 1 f 13/13 $106.66
PAMPTE PE, John 63 m 14/14 $106.66
        Mary wife 45 f 15/15 $106.66
        Mackie or Harry son 31 m 16/16 $106.66
        George son 28 m 17/17 $106.66
        Samuel son 17 m 18/18 $106.66
        Warren son 13 m 19/19 $106.66
PAMPTE PE, John, Jr. 30 m 20/20 $106.66
        Jane wife 31 f 21/21 $106.66
        Mary dau 7 f 22/22 $106.66
        Angeline dau 4 f 23/23 $106.66
        Cyrus son 2wk m -/-
KETOSH, Henry 22 m 24/24 $106.66
        Samuel bro 18 m 25/25 $106.66
        Charlotte sis 14 f 26/26 $106.67
```

SAW-GO-QUOT, Mackie 62 m 27/27 $106.67
    John son 25 m 28/28 $106.67
    Augustus son 22 m 29/29 $106.67
    Thomas son 18 m 30/30 $106.67
POKAGON, Jennie 7 f 31/31 $106.67 Rem: gdau of #27
MANDOKAY, Charlotte 57 f 33/32 $106.67
MANDOKAY, Samuel 24 m 34/33 $106.67
    Jane wife 21 f 35/34 $106.67
    Nancy dau 1 f 36/35 $106.67
MANDOKAY, Joseph, Jr. 30 m 37/36 $106.67
    Eliza wife 23 f 38/37 $106.67
    John son 9 m 39/38 $106.67
    Joseph son 5 m 40/39 $106.67
    Angeline dau 2 f 41/40 $106.67
WAY-NA-WEH 41 m 42/41 $106.67
    Josephine wife 36 f 43/42 $106.67
    John son 14 m 44/43 $106.67
    Peter son 9 m 45/44 $106.67
    William son 6 m 46/45 $106.67
    Phoeba dau 1 f 47/46 $106.67
E-DO-WE-GE-ZHICK 74 m 49/47 $106.67
    Nancy wife 56 f 50/48 $106.67
    Isaac son 16 m 51/49 $106.67
NAW-NAW-QUABE (Stephen Mackie) 35 m 52/50 $106.67
    Maun-go-quoi wife 38 f 53/51 $106.67
    Elizabeth dau 8 f 54/52 $106.67
    Jeff son 5 m 55/53 $106.67
NOON-WEH, Jacob 28 m 56/54 $106.67
    Lucy wife 26 f 57/55 $106.67
    Jacob, Jr. 1 m -/56 $106.67
WEE-ZOO, Thomas 48 m 58/57 $106.67
    Rosa wife 40 f 59/58 $106.67
    Addie dau 19 f 60/59 $106.67
    Eunice dau 15 f 61/60 $106.67
    Mary dau 11 f 62/61 $106.67
    Agnes dau 8 f 63/62 $106.67
    Nancy dau 2 f 64/63 $106.67
WEE-ZOO, Mary Ann 29 f 66/64 $106.67
    Martha dau 8 f 67/65 $106.67
    Francis son 6 m 68/66 $106.67
    Peter son 1 m 69/67 $106.67
MUN-QUA-TE-NAH (Wallace Hinman) 41 m -/-
    Mary wife 41 f 70/68 $106.67
WATSON, Amos 42 m 71/69 $106.67
    Elizabeth wife 43 f 72/70 $106.67
    Etta Alice dau 9 f 73/71 $106.67
    Nancy Jennie dau 4 f 74/72 $106.67
    Sarah Ann dau 1 f 75/73 $106.67
AISH-KE-BA, Francis 67 m 76/- Rem: name carried on
        former rolls but not entitled to payment

ISAAC, Sarah 45 f 77/74 $106.67
    Nancy dau 12 f 78/75 $106.67

1895 CENSUS OF AUGUST 5TH
POTTAWATOMI OF INDIANA & MICHIGAN

SIN-GO-WAW & Wife #1/- Rem: both deceased
MIX, John m 80 #2/1 Res: Hartford, MI
    Elizabeth 2nd wife f 50 #-/2 Rem: dau of #1
BOURASSA, Julia f 48 -/3 Res: North Arauar Co., MI
    Rem: dau of #2
MIX, Lawrence m 30 #-/4 Res: Hartford, MI Rem: son
    of #2
    R. C. son m 12 #-/5
    L. P. son m 9 #-/6
MIX, William m 33 #-/7 Res: Hartford, MI Rem: son of
    #2
    Agnes wife f 25 #-/8 Rem: dau of #23
MIX, John Jr. m 25 #-/9 Res: Hartford, MI Rem: son
    of #2
BIRD, Lena f 12 #-/10 Res: Kalkaska, MI Rem: dau of
    9 & gdau of #2
    Bessie sis f 10 #-/11
CUSHWAY, Angeline f 45 #-/12 Res: Fern, MI Rem: wife
    of 215 & dau of #2
    Clara A. dau f 19 #-/13
    Chas. H. son m 16 #-/14
    James E. son m 12 #-/15
    Annie C. dau f 7 #-/16
RIDER, Martha A. f 25 #-/17 Res: Fern, MI Rem: dau
    of 12
    J. Emory son m 4 #-/18
    John A. son m 2 #-/19
BUSHAW, Nora J. f 23 #-/20 Res: Fern, MI Rem: dau of
    12
    Joseph son m 2 #-/21
WILSON, Mary f 21 #-/22 Res: Fern, MI Rem: dau of 12
NAW-GE-ZHE-YAW, Winchester #3/- Rem: dec'd; on
    old roll had wife & 5 children, all are
    dead except one child
KING, Mary Josephine f 49 #-/23 Res: Dowagiac, MI
    Rem: widow no children; dau of #3
WINCHESTER, Anna f 40 #-/24 Res: Dowagair, MI Rem:
    widow of John Winchester, dec'd; dau of #4
    Thomas son m 21 #-/25
QUAY-GO-NO (Quigano), John m 64 #4/26 Res: Hartford,
    MI Rem: wife dead
    Dominick son m 15 #-/27 Rem: at Haskell Inst.

73

QUAY-GO-NO, Isaac m 40 #-/28 Res: Hartford, MI Rem:
        son of #4
    Michael son m 20 #-/29
    Julia dau f 17 #-/30
    Francis son 9 #-/31
    Sarah dau 7 #-/32
QUAY-GO-NO, John Jr. m 33 #-/33 Res: Hartford, MI
        Rem: son of #4
    Angeline wife f 26 #-/34 Rem: dau of #14
    Elizabeth dau f 11 #-/35
    Mary dau f 9 #-/36
    Louisa dau f 4 #-/37
    Peter son m 2 #-/38
    Henry son m 10mo #-/39
BATTICE, William m 40 #-/40 Res: Lake City, MI Rem:
        son of #67
    Terresa 2nd wife f 21 #-/41 Rem: dau of #4
    Mary dau f 6 #-/42
    Daniel son m 4 #-/43
    Alice dau f 2 #-/44
    Nancy dau f 1 #-/45
    Frank son m 15 #-/46 Rem: child by 1st wife
    Joseph son m 13 #-/47 Rem: child by 1st wife
    Henry son m 11 #-/48 Rem: child by 1st wife
WAUB-SEIGH & Wife #5/- Rem: wife & 4 children old
        roll dead
WOPSEE, Frank Wuicheseya m 51 #-/49 Res: Walpole
        Island, Algonas, MI Rem: son of #5
SANDS, Mary Ann f 21 #-/50 Res: Algonas, MI Rem: dau
        of 49
    Ester dau f 5 #-/51
KAW-GAIBE, Susan f 12 #-/52 Rem: father's name is
        George Kaw-gaibe lives near Mt. Pleasant,
        MI, mother now deceased was dau of #5
    John bro m 10 #-/53
O-SKE-NAW-WAY #6/- Rem dec'd; wife & 3 children old
        roll dead
O-SKE-NAW-WAY (SKIUWAY), Mary f 20 #-/54 Res:
        Hartford, MI Rem: dau of #6
    Louis son M 7 #-/55 Rem: illegitimate
O-SKE-NAW-WAY (SKIUWAY), Angeline f 12 #-/56 Res:
        Hartford, MI Rem: gdau of #6; child of
        Alexis Skiuway, dec'd
O-SKE-NAW-WAY (SKIUWAY), Alexander m 50 #-/57 Res:
        Hart, MI Rem: son of #6
KAW-KAW-KAW-SHE & Wife #7/- Rem: deceased
COWLES, Edward B. m 48 #-/58 Res: Fairbury, NE Rem:
        son of #7
COWLES, Helen Elizabeth f 50 #-/59 Res: 1609 South
        9th St., Council Bluffs, IA Rem: dau of #7

RAPP, George m 83 #8/60 Res: 1609 South 9th St.,
    Council Bluffs, IA Rem: son of #7
    Cecelia dau f 17 #-/61
RAPP, Andrew m 31 #-/62 Res: Bower, NE Rem: son of
    #7
RAPP, Anthony m 33 #-/63 Res: Fairbury, NE Rem: son
    of #7
    Joseph son m 13 #-/64
    William son m 9 #-/65
RAPP, David m 39 #-/66 Res: Lake City, MI Rem: son
    of #8
    Mary wife f 38 #-/67 Rem: dau of #22
    Maggie dau f 16 #-/68
    Lizzie dau f 14 #-69
    Loyal dau f 12 #-/70
    Cecelia dau f 10 #-/71
    Victoria dau f 8 #-72
    John son m 6 #-/73
    Jennie dau f 4 #-/74
WEZO-MOTAY m 70 #9/75 Res: Hartford, MI Rem: wife
    & 3 children old roll dead
MOTAY, Joseph m 51 #-/76 Res: Hartford, MI Rem: son
    of #9 & drew on old roll as Joseph Motay &
    #36 are one and the same person (Key-tosh
    #36)
    Elizabeth wife f 50 #-/77
    Louis son m 12 #-/78
    Agnes dau f 10 #-/79
    Annie dau f 8 #-80
    David son m 5 #-/81
MOTAY, Basil m 25 #-/82 Res: Hartford, MI Rem: son
    of 76; now at Haskell Inst.
MOTAY, Charles m 21 #-/83 Res: Hartford, MI Rem: son
    of 76
BLACKMAN, Sophia f 29 #-/84 Res: Hartford, MI Rem:
    dau of 76
    Louis son m 5 #-/85
    Peter son m 5mo #-/86
WAW-O-GIN m 75 #10/87 Res: Lake City, MI Rem: dec'd;
    wife on old roll dead
WAGIN, John m 36 #-/88 Res: Saugatuck, MI Rem:
    descendant of #10
    Benjamin son m 12 #-/89 Rem: lives with Simon
        Pokagon at Lee, MI
    Francis son m 10 #-/90 Rem: lives with Simon
        Pokagon at Lee, MI
KECHE-SETHONE #11/- Rem: dec'd; wife & 3 children on
    old roll are dead
SETONE, Isaac m 35 #-/91 Res: Hartford, MI Rem:
    descendant of #11

Angelina wife f 27 #-/92 Rem: dau of #8
Lawrence son m 6 #-/93
Louis son m 3 #-/94
KECHE-NAY-GO m 70 #12/95 Res: Hartford, MI Rem: now
        ALEXIS, Chenigar; wife & one child on old
        roll dead
ALEXIS, David m 40 #-/96 Res: South Bend, IN Rem:
        son of #12; all the sons took Alexis as
        surname, now the father has taken the name
        of Alexis as surname see #12
    Arthur son m 13 #-/97
    Samuel son m 11 #-/98
    Robert son m 7 #-/99
    Mary Eliz. dau f 2 #-/100
ALEXIS, Patrick m 32 #-/101 Res: Hartford, MI Rem:
        son of #12
    Betsey wife f 38 #-/102 Rem: dau of #8
    Charles son m 18 #-/103
    Henry son m 10 #-/104
    Leo son m 6 #-/105
    St. Patrick m 1mo #-/106
ALEXIS, Michael m 45 #-/107 Res: Hartford, MI Rem:
        son of #12
    Elizabeth dau f 17 #-/108
    Louisa dau f 13 #-/109
    Nora dau f 1 #-/110
LEWIS, Mary f 28 #-/111 Res: Hartford, MI Rem: dau
        of #12
    Ida dau f 10 #-/112
    William son m 7 #-/113
    Jacob son m 5 #-/114
    Martha dau f 3 #-115
    Julia dau f 1 #-/116
O-GE-MAW-WE #13/- Rem: dec'd; wife & 4 children old
        roll dead
MAWSO, Joseph #14/- Rem: dec'd; wife & one child old
        roll; another child see 262
SAUGMA, Nancy f 40 #-/117 Res: Hamilton, MI Rem: dau
        of #14
MAWSO, Peter m 38 #-/118 Res: Hamilton, MI Rem: deaf
        & dumb; son of #14
    Thereasa dau f 1 #-/119
GIBSON, Mary Elizabeth f 36 #-/120 Res: Hamilton, MI
        Rem: dau of #14
    Martha dau f 7 #-/121
    James son m 5 #-/122
    Isaac son m 2 #-/123
MAWSO, Alexis m 32 #-/124 Res: Kalkaska, MI Rem: son
        of #14
    Martha dau f 13 #-/125

MAWSO, Daniel m 21 #-/126 Res: Hartford, MI Rem:
        child of Joe Waw-saw now dead & grandchild
        of #14
    Mary sis f 16 #-/127
    Louisa sis f 14 #-/128
    Edward M. bro m 3 #-/129
MAWSO, Louisa f 25 #-/130 Res: Hamilton, MI Rem: dau
        of #14
WALKER, Mary f 23 #-/131 Res: Kalkaska, MI Rem: dau
        of #14
    Martha dau f 6 #-/132
    Angeline dau f 4 #-/133
    (Infant) son m 2 #-134
AKEN #15/- Rem: deceased
AKEN GREEN, Mary f 60 #-/135 Res: Lake City, MI Rem:
        wife of #15; three of four children on old
        roll are dead
    Paul son m 17 #-/136
POKAGON, Alexander m 40 #-/137 Res: Salem, MI Rem:
        son of #15
    Joseph son m 12 #-/138
    William son m 7 #-/139
    White Pigeon son m 1 #-/140
WILLIAMS (Kow-tuck-mock), William m 75 #16/141 Res:
        Hartford, MI Rem: 3 of the children on old
        roll are dead
    Elizabeth wife f 55 #-/142
    Michael son m 15 #-/143
WILLIAMS, Peter m 29 #-/144 Res: Hartford, MI Rem:
        son of #16; single
WILLIAMS, Frank m 25 #-/145 Res: Hartford, MI Rem:
        son of #16; single
WILLIAMS, John m 23 #-/146 Res: Hartford, MI Rem:
        son of #16; single
WILLIAMS, Angeline f 21 #-/147 Res: Hartford, MI
        Rem: dau of #16; single
PARSONS, Mrs. Levi #17/- Rem: deceased
PARSONS, Joseph m 41 #-/148 Res: Buchanan, MI Rem:
        son of #17
    Frank son m 11 #-/149
    Nora dau f 9 #-/150
PARSONS, Louis m 39 #-/151 Res: Buchanan, MI Rem:
        son of #17
PARSONS, Charles m 31 #-/152 Res: Buchanan, MI Rem:
        son of #17
PARSONS, Peter m 25 #-/153 Res: Buchanan, MI Rem:
        son of #17
TOPOSH, Mary f 37 #-/154 Res: Dowagiac, MI Rem: wife
        of 258; dau of #17; wife of #55
    Louis son m 8 #-/155

Levi son m 6 #-/156
Cecelia dau f 3 #-/157
Joseph son m 18mo #-/158
TOPOSH, Cecelia Sarah f 28 #-/159 Res: Dowagiac, MI
Rem: wife of 259; dau of #17
Agnes dau f 1 #-/160
AW-QUE-WE-NAW #18/- Rem: deceased; had five children
all dead but Agnes
KNAPP, Agnes f 45 #-/161 Res: Benton Harbor, MI Rem:
dau of #18
Joseph son m 25 #-/162 Rem: in Michigan City,
IN prison; illegitimate
Paul son m 8 #-/163
AUGUSTUS, Wm. & Wife #19/- Rem: both deceased
AUGUSTUS, Joseph m 34 #-/164 Res: Dowagiac, MI Rem:
son of #19; single
AUGUSTUS, Isaac m 32 #-/165 Res: Dowagiac, MI Rem:
son of #19; single; now at Haskell Inst.
MOOSE, Lawrence m 36 #-/166 Res: Dowagiac, MI
Rem: son of #19 by first husb & gson of
#52; single
POKAGON, Simon m 65 #20/167 Res: Lee, MI Rem: two
children on old roll dead
Victoria wife f 50 #-/168 Rem: dau of #4
POKAGON, William m 28 #-/169 Res: Lee, MI Rem: son
of #20
Lizette wife f 25 #-/170 Rem: dau of #14
Julia dau f 13 #-/171
Mary dau f 11 #-/172
Cecelia dau f 2 #-/173
Jewitt son m 3mo #-/174
POKAGON, Charles L. m 26 #-/175 Res: Lee, MI Rem:
son of #20
Angeline wife f 28 #-/- Rem: not elligible, dau
of Pew-so-quah who died before 1866
Josephine dau f 14 #-/176
Elizabeth dau f 8 #-/177
Lucy dau f 6 #-/178
O-SAW-GE-QUAY #21/- Rem: dec'd; two children on old
roll are dead
BUSH, Mary f 41 #-/179 Res: Hamilton, MI Rem: dau of
#21
Frank son m 18 #-/180
Foster son m 14 #-/181
Joshua son m 6 #-/182
Silas son m 2 #-/183
THOMPSON, Mary f 61 #-/184 Res: Dowagiac, MI Rem:
two Marys but both (half sisters) said to
be daughters of #21

TAW-CAW-MAW-GAY #22/- Rem: dec'd; one child on old
    roll dead
    Mary wife f 65 Res: Hamilton, MI #-/185
TAW-CAW-MAW-GAY, Paul m 45 #-/186 Res: Hamilton, MI
    Rem: son of #22
    John son m 16 #-/187
    Nora dau f 11 #-/188
    Martha dau f 9 #-189
    James son m 7 #-190
    Minnie dau f 5 #-/191
    Daniel son m 3 #-/192
SETHONE the 2nd #23/- Rem: dec'd; wife & 2 children
    dead; one child is wife of 7
POKAGON, James #24/- Rem: dec'd; wife & 3 children
    dead
HAMILTON, Frank m 19 #-/193 Res: Dowagiac, MI Rem:
    gson of #24
MAW-NE-DO-QUE-SAUSE #25/- Rem: dec'd; wife & 2
    children on old roll dead
WHITE, Sarah f 30 #-/194 Res: South Bend, IN Rem:
    gdau of #25
    (Infant) dau f 1 #-/195
SHAWNON, Louisa f 26 #-/196 Res: Lawpasas, TX Rem:
    gdau of #25
MENISH, Jerome m 21 #-/197 Res: Hartford, MI Rem:
    gson of #25
NAW-GEE, Marion (Mrs. Joe Bevins) f 56 #26/198 Res:
    Hamilton, MI Rem: two children on old roll
    dead
GEZICK, Elizabeth (Mrs. John) f 33 #-/199 Res:
    Wallin, MI Rem: dau of #26; two more
    children 269 & 270
    Angeline dau f 18 #-/200
    Cecelia gdau f 4 #-/201 Rem: illegitimate dau
    of Angeline
    Agnes gdau f 2 #-/202 Rem: illegitimate dau of
    Angeline
    Julia dau f 10 #-/203
    Lucy dau f 7 #-/204
    Sullivan son m 5 #-/205
RIFFLE, Joseph m 10 #-/206 Res: Stetson, MI Rem:
    gson of #26; child of Nancy Riffle now
    dead who was the dau of #26
    George bro m 8 #-/207
TEQUON, Joseph m 70 #27/208 Res: Hartford, MI Rem:
    wife & 1 child old roll dead
TEQUON, Dominick m 25 #-/209 Res: Hartford, MI Rem:
    son of #27
MICK-SE-MOCK #28/- Rem: dec'd; wife and 1 child on
    old roll dead

79

MICK-SE-MOCK, Mary Jane f 22 #-/210 Res: Hartford,
    MI Rem: now at Haskell Inst.; dau of #28
SHERBORN, Louis m 21 #-/211 Res: Hartford, MI Rem:
    now at Haskell Inst.; gson of #28
KE-NO-NAW-NE-QUAY #29/- Rem: dec'd
PEPPEYAR, Stephen m 37 #-/212 Res: Athens, MI Rem:
    gson of #29
CUSHWAY, Joe H. m 45 #-/213 Res: Fern, MI Rem: said to
    have been adopted son of #29 & drew in 1866;
    see 12 for family
LEWIS, Alexis m 37 #-/214 Res: Fern, MI Rem: said to
    have been adopted son of #29 & drew in 1866
    Joseph son m 6 #-/215
    (Infant) son m 3mo #-/216
MAW-CHE-WE-TAW #30/- Rem: dec'd; wife & one child on
    old roll dead
ME-SQUAW-BAW-NO-QUAY #31/- Rem: dec'd; two children on
    old roll also dead
AISH-KE-BE #32/- Rem: dec'd; wife is dead; the one
    child was adopted & was Wm. Battise
    accounted for with #4
MAY-ME-GWE #33/- Rem: dec'd; wife is dead
AUGUSTUS, Madeline f 38 #-/217 Res: Dowagiac, MI Rem:
    dau of #33; wife of #47
    William son m 19 #-/218
    Mary dau f 16 #-/219
    Lucy Silas dau f #-/220
    Sarah dau f #-/221
PE-QUAW-CO-SAY #34/- Rem: dec'd; wife dead
PEW-TO-PE, Josephine f 38 #-/222 Res: Athens, MI Rem:
    dau of #34
KAW-O-GO-MO (WILLIAMS), Frank m 62 #35/223 Res:
    Hamilton, MI Rem: his wife is now the wife
    of Simon Pokagon & the child on old roll is
    dead
KEY-TOSH #36/- Rem: see 76 Joseph Motay are the same
    & one person
RAIL, Antoine #37/- Rem: dec'd
TOPOSH, Angeline f 52 #-/224 Res: Dowagiac, MI Rem:
    dau of #37
RAIL, Elizabeth f 52 #-/225 Res: Dowagiac, MI Rem: dau
    of #37
KE-NE-SO-QUAY #38/- Rem: dec'd; on old roll one son
    dead
PAY-CO-SAW #39/- Rem: dec'd; on old roll one child a
    son dead
WEZO, Louis m 51 #40/226 Res: Hartford, MI Rem: wife
    is dead
NAW-O-KEE #41/- Rem: dec'd; wife is dead
SO-ZETTE #42/- Rem: dec'd

80

BATTISE, Nancy f 30 #-/227 Res: Fern, MI Rem: raised
          & adopted child, a grand neice of wife of
          Louis Battise
KE-CHE-WEZO #43/- Rem: dec'd
WEZO, Francis m 23 #-/228 Res: Hartford, MI Rem:
          called Big Wezo; son of #43
WEZO, James m 21 #-/229 Res: Hartford, MI Rem: son of
          #43
KEZ-HICK #44/- Rem: dec'd
SOLOMON, Mary f 64 #-/230 Res: Hamilton, MI Rem: was
          wife of #44, now wife of David Solomon
SIN-GO-QUAY #45/- Rem: dec'd; old roll one child now
          dead
BAZIL, Mary #46/- Rem: dec'd
BAZIL, Neyoe m 45 #-/231 Res: Dowagiac, MI Rem: son of
          #46
     Alice wife f 44 #-/232 Rem: gdau of #21
     Jane dau f 20 #-/233
     Charles son m 18 #-/234
     Louis son m 16 #-/235
     Elizabeth dau f 13 #-/236
     Sarah dau f 11 #-/237
     Mary dau f 8 #-/238
PE-WAW-QUS-NUM, Augusta f 80 #47/239 Res: Dowagiac, MI
AUGUSTA, John m 48 #-/240 Res: Dowagiac, MI Rem: wife
          see 217; now in prison at Jackson, MI; son
          of #47
BAZIL, John #48/- Rem: dec'd
WATSON, Elizabeth f 49 #-/241 Res: Athens, MI Rem: 1st
          husb #48, now wife of Watson
BAZIL, Henry m 23 #-/242 Res: Athens, MI Rem: son of
          #48 & 241
WATSON, Nancy Jane f 10 #-/243 Res: Athens, MI Rem:
          dau of 241
     Sarah Ann sis f 8 #-/244
BAZIL, Agnes f 26 #-/245 Res: Athens, MI Rem: dau of
          #48 & 241
     Margaret dau f 3 #-/246
POKAGON, Lawrence #49/- Rem: dec'd; wife on old roll
          also dead
POKAGON, Edward m 25 #-/247 Res: Sacred Heart Mission,
          OK
POKAGON, Francis #50/- Rem: dec'd
POKAGON, Betsey f 70 #-/248 Res: Crumstown, IN Rem:
          widow of #50
BURELL, Mary Eliz. f 50 #-/249 Res: Crumstown, IN Rem:
          dau of #50
BLACKMAN, Joseph m 32 #-/250 Res: Hartford, MI Rem:
          son of 249

81

DIXON, Martha f 29 #-/251 Res: Hartford, MI Rem: dau
     of 249
     Eliza Jane dau f 11 #-/252
     Cora dau f 9 #-/253
     Lucy dau f 7 #-/254
     Jane dau f 5 #-/255
DOMINICK #51/- Rem: dec'd
MOOSE #52/- Rem: dec'd
ANSE, Mrs. Antoine #53/- Rem: dec'd
ANSE, Peter m 27 #-/256 Res: Dowagiac, MI Rem: son of
     #53; no children
ANSE, John m 25 #-/257 Res: Dowagiac, MI Rem: now at
     Haskell Inst; son of #53
CUSHWAY, John #54/- Rem: dec'd
TOPOSH, Mawnee #55/- Rem: dec'd; husb of 154
TOPOSH, Thomas m 36 #-/258 Res: Dowagiac, MI Rem: son
     of #55; wife see 154
TOPOSH, Daniel m 27 #-/259 Res: Dowagiac, MI Rem: son
     of #55; wife see 154
TOPOSH, Theresa f 25 #-/260 Res: Dowagiac, MI Rem: dau
     of #55; not married
AUGUUSTA, Louis #56/- Rem: dec'd
BATTISE, Peter #57/- Rem: dec'd
BATTISE, John #58/261 Res: Hartford, MI Rem: known as
     "Shobtise" or John Blackman
SAW-GO-MAW-QUAY #59/- Rem: dec'd
MAISH-QUOS #60/- Rem: dec'd
WAW-GO-KO-WE-NAW, Mrs. #61/- Rem: dec'd
JACKSON #62/- Rem: dec'd
O-GE-MAW-QUAY #63/- Rem: dec'd
KAW-KEE, Joseph #64/- Rem: dec'd
WAW-SO #65/- Rem: dec'd
SIN-GO-WAW, Elizabeth Rem: see wife of #2
WAW-SAW-TOE #-/- Rem: dec'd, son of #14; has a
     grandchild Wm. Battise see 40; for children
     see 126. 127, 128 & 129
POKAGON, Angeline f 28 #-/- Res: Lee, MI
AIKEN, Eliza f 17 #-/- Res: Newaygo, MI Rem: dau of
     preceeding Angeline Pokagon
MAWSO, Alice f 21 #-/262 Res: Hamilton, MI Rem: dau of
     #14
COWLES, Calvin C. m 43 #-/263 Res: 1609 South 9th St.,
     Council Bluffs, IA Rem: son of #7
     Zula dau f 11 #-/264
     Lela dau f 9 #-/265
     Pearl Lorain dau f 7 #-/266
COWLES, Arron H. m 32 #-/267 Res: Bower, NE Rem: son
     of #7
COWLES, Harriet f 38 #-/268 Res: Fairbury, NE Rem: dau
     of #7

GEZICK, Tier m 3 #-269 Res: Wallice, MI Rem: son of
    199
    Awaso bro m 1 #-/270

1904 TAGGART CENSUS ROLL
POTAWATOMI OF MICHIGAN

MENDOKAY, Samuel 41 m #1 Res: Athens, Mich.
    Mary wife 36 f #2 Rem: dau of Betsey Walker #12
    Ida sdau 18 f #3 Rem: dau of #2
    Gayley son 13 m #4
    Grover son 7 m #5
    Austin son 6 m #6
MENDOKAY, Joseph 47 m #7 Res: Athens, Mich.
    Caroline wife 50 f #8 Rem: dau of #12; on
        schedule as Walker but now married
    Frank son 20 m #9
    Angeline dau f #10
    George son m #11
WALKER, Betsey 65 f #12 Res: Bradley, Mich. Rem: Geo
    Walker a son was entitled to enrollment but
    by mistake his name not included in those
    passed upon on the court of Claims his right
    was however proved up his claimed see #268
    Solomon 39 son #13
    Jacob 32 son #14
    William son m #15 Res: Wayland, Mich.
    Hiram son m #16 Res: Wayland, Mich.
WEZOO, Thomas 65 m #17 Res: Athens, Mich.
    Rosa wife 60 f #18 Rem: sis of #27 & #22
    Elizabeth dau f #19
    Lucy dau f #20
    Mary dau 30 f #21 Rem: name now is Mary Bazil or
        Mrs. Henry Bazil
JOHNSON, James 34 m #22 Res: Athens, Mich. Rem: bro of
    #18 & #27
    Martha Shaw-go-quot wife f #23
    Angeline dau f #24
    Louis son m #25
    Mary dau f #26
SHA-GO-NA-BY, Mrs. Joseph 60 f #27 Res: Athens, Mich.
    Rem: husb not on roll
    John son 28 m #28 Res: Hamilton, Mich.
    William son m #29 Res: Hamilton, Mich.
    George son m #30
    Lydian dau f #31 Res: Hamilton, Mich.
    Charley son m #32
    Isaac son m #33
    Alexander m #34 Res: Hamilton, Mich. Rem: dec'd

83

MEDAWIS, Mrs. Peter 60 f #35 Res: Hamilton, Mich. Rem:
        sis of #18; husb not on this roll
    Mary dau f #36
    Hannah dau f #37
SPRAGUE, Selkerk 35 m #38 Res: Bradley, Mich. Rem: son
        of Alice Jackson #189, one of the 7 of her
        children
    Helen wife 34 f #39 Rem: dau of Helen Medawis
        #35, so named on claim
MEDAWIS, Johnson 22 m #40 Res: Hamilton, Mich. Rem:
        son of #35; wife not on this roll
PIGEON, Sampson 30 m #41 Res: Hamilton, Mich. Rem: son
        of #35 by Wm Pigeon
    Eliza wife 17 f #42 Rem: dau of #126
MARK, Mrs. Alfred 34 f #43 Res: Allegan, Mich. Rem:
        husb not on this roll
    Albert son m #44
    Angeline dau f #45
    Jennie dau f #46
SIN-O-QUAY 39 f #47 Res: Free Soil, Mich. Rem: husb
        not on this roll
    James son 10 m #48
    Paul son 7 m #49
PAMP-TO-PE, John 78 m #50 Res: Athens, Mich. Rem: wife
            #89
    Henry son 51 m #51
    Samuel son 34 m #52
    George son 36 m #53
    John gson 6 m #54 Rem: son of #53
    John neph m #55 Rem: son of #58
PAMP-TO-PE, Phineas 68 m #56 Res: Athens, Mich. Rem:
        bro of #50
    Rodney son 49 m #57
    Frank son 40 m #58
    Jacob son 37 m #59
    George son 35 m #60
    Stephen son 32 m #61 Rem: husb of #91
    Mary Ann gdau f #62 Rem: dau of #61
    Johnny neph 49 m #63 Rem: son of #50
    Mrs. Jane 50 f #64 Rem: wife of #63
    Mary 22 f #65 Res: Hartford, Mich. Rem: dau of
        #64; husb not on roll; now named Mrs. Chas.
        We-saw
    Angeline 18 f #66 Rem: dau of #64
    Silas 16 m #67 Res: Athens, Mich. Rem: son of #64
    Levi 13 m #68 Rem: son of #64
    Elizabeth 9 f #69 Rem: dau of #64
    Phineas m #70 Rem: dead; son of #64
SHAW-GO-QUOT, Mee-Me 72 m #71 Res: Athens, Mich.
    Mackey 85 m #72

MEE-ME, Joseph 41 m #73 Res: Athens, Mich. Rem: son of
       #71
MACKEY, Mary 60 f #74 Res: Athens, Mich. Rem: died Jul
       15, 1903
    John son 41 m #75
    Gus son 38 m #76
JOHNSON, Jennie 22 f #77 Res: Athens, Mich. Rem: gdau
       of #72
ALEXIS, Mrs. Mary 48 f #78 Res: Hartford, Mich. Rem:
       dau of #71; husb not on Schedule "A"
    Thomas son 21 m #79 Rem: or We-saw; son of #78 by
       former husb, see #77 payroll vou 7 Spec.
       Agt. Taggart 1905
EDWARD, Isaac 20 m #80 Res: Hartford, Mich. Rem: son
       of #23; gson of #71
CAW-CAW-BE, William 76 m #81 Res: Athens, Mich.
BIRCH, Henry 30 m #82 Res: Athens, Mich.
    Mary L. wife 34 f #83 Rem: nee Caw-caw-be, dau of
       #81
NOTTAWAY, David 63 m #84 Res: Athens, Mich.
    Josephine wife 50 f #85
    Peter son 26 m #86
    William son 21 m #87
    Samuel son 16 m #88
PAMP-TO-PEE, Mrs. Mary 70 f #89 Res: Athens, Mich.
       Rem: was wife of #50
WATSON, Amos 59 m #90 Res: Athens, Mich.
PAMP-TO-PEE, Mrs. Agnes 24 f #91 Res: Athens, Mich.
       Rem: wife of #61
COB-COB-MO-SA, Mary 62 f #92 Res: Athens, Mich.
DAVID, James 63 m #93 Res: Athens, Mich.
    Sarah wife 68 f #94
MACKETY, Albert m #95 Res: Athens, Mich. Rem: gson of
       #93
    Betsey sis f #96 Rem: gdau of #93
MO-GWAW-GO, George 65 m #97 Res: Hamilton, Mich.
MACKEY, Mrs. Ida 32 f #98 Res: Wayland, Mich. Rem:
       wife of Solomon Walker; died Jan 1904
    Frank son m #99
    Alice dau f #100
ISAAC, Mrs. Sarah 63 f #101 Res: Athens, Mich. Rem:
       sis of #93
PEPEYAR, Emma 34 f #102 Res: Athens, Mich. Rem: niece
       of #93
    Paul son 8 m #103
    Elizabeth dau 5 f #104
WAKAZOO, Joseph 60 m #105 Res: Lengby Polk Co., Minn.
WAKAZOO, Moses 55 m #106 Res: Petoskey, Mich. Rem: bro
       of #105 & #107

WAKAZOO, John 52 m #107 Res: Northport, Mich. Rem: bro
    of #105 & #106
    Moses son 30 m #108
    Amos son 28 m #109
    Anna dau 25 f #110
    Susan dau f #111
AUGOSA, Mrs. David 68 f #112 Res: Northport, Mich.
    Jacob son 48 m #113
    Paul son 45 m #114
    Robert son 42 m #115
ASH-QUAB, Moses 58 m #116 Res: Mt. Pleasant, Mich.
    Charlie son 23 m #117
    Sarah dau f #118
    Priscilla dau f #119
WALKER, Mrs. George 34 f #120 Res: Mt. Pleasant, Mich.
    Rem: dau of #116; see #268
JOHN, Betsey 45 f #121 Res: Mt. Pleasant, Mich.
BENNETT, David 48 m #122 Res: Mt. Pleasant, Mich. Rem:
    neph of #116
PUSH-KISH-GO-QUAY 72 f #123 Res: Wayland, Mich. Rem:
    Executor of will & estate
FOX, David 55 m #124 Res: Bradley, Mich. Rem: son of
    #123
    Adam son 21 m #125
MEDAWIS, Mrs. Lewis 57 f #126 Res: Bradley, Mich. Rem:
    sis of #124
    Sarah dau 24 f #127
    Henry son m #128 Res: Burnips Corners, Mich.
    Wm McKinley son m #129 Res: Burnips Corners,
    Mich.
FOSTER, James 33 m #130 Res: Bradley, Mich. Rem: son
    of #200
    Nancy wife 22 f #131 Rem: nee Medawis; dau of #
    126; on schedule as Medawis
PIGEON, James 43 m #132 Res: Burnips Corners, Mich.
    Rem: bro of #136
    Mrs. James wife 41 f #133
    Sarah dau f #134
    Jane dau f #135
PIGEON, John 31 m #136 Res: Burnips Corners, Mich.
    Rem: bro of #132
    Mrs. John wife 30 f #137
    Wallace son m #138
    Rosa dau f #139
THOMPSON, Peter 59 m #140 Res: Fountain, Mich.
POKAGON, Lucy 45 f #141 Res: Burnips Corners, Mich.
    Rem: sis of #132 & #136
    Elliott son m #142
    Peter son m #143

SAWS-WAY, John 62 m #144 Res: Mt. PLeasant, Mich.
    Nuck-quot son m #145
FRANS-WAY, Levi 43 m #146 Res: Mt. Pleasant, Mich.
        Rem: son of #144; correct name is Saws-way
        but answers also to name herein written
    Alice dau f #147
    Jennie dau f #148
    John son m m #149
PE-NAS-SE-WAH-NO-QUAY 42 f #150 Res: Mt. Pleasant,
        Mich. Rem: dau of #144
PAY-CO-TUSH, Samuel 60 m #151 Res: Mt. Pleasant, Mich.
        Rem: hbro of #144
NA-SE-WE-DIN-O-QUAY 60 f #152 Res: Mt. Pleasant, Mich.
        Rem: wife of #116
PAY-SHE-GE-ZHICK 58 m #153 Res: Edward Center, Mich.
        Rem: bro of #155; English name is Henry
        McClure & is also known by that name
        generally
SHAW-O-SE-GE-ZHICK 50 m #154 Res: Mt. Pleasant, Mich.
MCCLURE, William 50 m #155 Res: Mt. Pleasant, Mich.
        Rem: bro of #153
    Jane dau 26 f #156
    Fred son 22 m #157
    Gus son m #158 Res: Hart, Mich.
MARSO, John m #159 Res: Douglas, Mich. Rem: adopted
        son of James Saw-ga-maw
CHIPPEWAY, William 60 m #160 Res: Mt. Pleasant, Mich.
    John son #161
    Walter son m #162
    Eliza dau f #163
NIN-WAY-QUAY 65 f #164 Res: Mt. Pleasant, Mich. Rem:
        widow
SHAW-BOOSE, Dan 40 m #165 Res: Mt. Pleasant, Mich.
        Rem: son of #164
    Harry son m #166
    Julia dau f #167
PAY-MAW-ME, Amos 45 m #168 Res: Mt. Pleasant, Mich.
    Albert bro 43 m #169
THOMAS, Lewis 43 m #170 Res: Mt. Pleasant, Mich.
KAY-KAKE, Edward 60 m #171 Res: Mt. Pleasant, Mich.
MOSIER, Andrew m #172 Res: Hamilton, Mich. Rem: gson
        of #171
KAY-KAKE, John 40 m #173 Res: Athens, Mich. Rem: son
        of #171
    Frank son m #174
KAY-KAKE, Isaac 55 m #175 Res: Athens, Mich. Rem: bro
        of #171
CHING-QUASH, Louis 34 m #176 Res: Lake City, Mich.
KE-WAY-JE-WAN 67 m #177 Res: Custer, Mich.
    Joseph son m #178

CHING-GWAN m #179 Res: Hart, Mich.
    George son 45 m #180 Res: Lattin, Mich.
PE-NAS-WA-GEE-SHICK m #181 Res: Mt. Pleasant, Mich.
    Rem: dec'd
SHA-GO-NA-BY, Kate 43 f #182 Res: Hamilton, Mich. Rem:
        wife of Chas. Rosoet, not on this roll
    Martha dau 22 f #183 Res: 85 Siverson St.,
        Detroit, Mich.; her present name is Martha
        Taylor
    Nancy dau f #184 Res: Hamilton, Mich.
    Eunice dau f #185
    Joshua son m #186
    Angeline dau f #187
HALFADAY, Abrim 48 m #188 Res: Hamilton, Mich. Rem:
        bro of #207
JACKSON, Alice 45 f #189 Res: Bradley, Mich. Rem: dau
        of #123; wife of Jacob Jackson, separated
SPRAUGE, Henry 22 m #190 Res: Bradley, Mich. Rem: son
        of #189
    James bro m #191 Res: Wayland, Mich.
JACKSON, Adam m #192 Res: Wayland, Mich. Rem: son of
        #189
    John A. bro m #193 Rem: dec'd
    Rosa sis f #194
NOON WEHR, Jacob m #195 Res: Athens, Mich. Rem: son of
        #189
CRAMPTON, Foster 45 m #196 Res: Custer, Mich.
    Lydia dau f #197
    James son m #198
    Lewis son m #199
FOSTER, David K. 65 m #200 Res: Shelbyville, Mich.
        Rem: bro of #205
    Charles son 44 m #201 Res: Bradley, Mich.
    Lincoln son 42 m #202
    Lucy dau 30 f #203
    Inman son 23 m #204
FOSTER, Moses 85 m #205 Res: Wayland, Mich. Rem: bro
        of #200; dec'd
MACTAY, Mrs. John f #206 Res: Athens, Mich. Rem: widow
HALFADAY, James 46 m #207 Res: Hamilton, Mich. Rem:
        bro of #188
    Nancy sis 48 f #208 Res: Athens, Mich.
    Albert son 23 m #209
    Mary dau 21 f #210 Rem: dec'd
SAW-GA-MAW, James 49 m #211 Res: Hamilton, MIch. Rem:
        wife not on roll
DAVID, Samuel 60 m #212 Res: Wayland, Mich. Rem: wife
        not on roll; dec'd
DAVID, Solomon 58 m #213 Res: Hamilton, Mich. Rem:
        wife not on roll; died June 1904

ENESS, William J. 48 m #214 Res: 3rd Ave. West of
        Ionia St., Grand Rapids, Mich. Rem: wife not
        on roll
    William J., Jr. son m #215
    Hazel dau f #216
    George son m #217
ENESS, Joseph 46 m #218 Res: Grand Rapids, Mich. Rem:
        bro of #214; wife, Harriet H. Eness, not on
        roll
    Clara dau f #219
ENESS, Lewis 43 m #220 Res: Grand Rapids, Mich. Rem:
        bro of #214 & #218
    Nellie dau f #221
    Eleanor dau f #222
ENESS, Enos 34 m #223 Res: 431 Turner St., Grand
        Rapids, Mich. Rem: bro of #214, #218 &
        #220; correct name is Amos L. Eness
    Harold L. son m #224
ENESS, Henry 32 m #225 Res: Grand Rapids, Mich. Rem:
        bro of #214, #218, #220 & #223
    Marguerite M. dau #226
ZOONDAH, James 63 m #227 Res: Lake City, Mich. Rem:
        bro of #230
KELSEY, Flora 15 f #228 Res: Mt. Pleasant, Mich. Rem:
        See testimony of James Zoondah & Judge
        Shipman & auth 92362; gdau of #227
    Johnnie bro 11 m #229
ZOONDAH, Cawsara m #230 Res: Lake City, Mich. Rem: bro
        of #227; dec'd
ZOONDAH, Levi 40 m #231 Res: Lake City, Mich.
    Willie son m #232
    Anna dau f #233
ZOONDAH, Peter m #234 Res: Lake City, Mich. Rem: bro
        of #231
JACKSON, Jacob 45 m #235 Res: Athens, Mich. Rem: husb
        of #189, separated
    Lucy wife 42 f #236 Rem: nee Kaykake, separated
BATTICE, John 50 m #237 Res: Custer, Mich.
    Lewis son 30 m #238
    Benedict son 28 m #239
    Joseph son 26 m #240
    Moses son 23 m #241
    Sha-ne-ya dau f #242 Rem: dec'd
SHA-SHA-GWAY, Mary 60 f #243 Res: Saugatuck, Mich.
        Rem: sis of #252 & #256
    Frances dau 30 f #244
    Joseph son 28 m #245
SHA-SHA-GWAY, William 40 m #246 Res: Holland, Mich.
        Rem: son of #243

Anna E. dau f #247 Res: 243 West 12th St.,
    Holland, Mich.
Joseph P. son m #248
Theresa E. dau f #249
Mary F. dau f #250
Agnes J. dau f #251
SNAY, Joseph 50 m #252 Res: Saugatuck, Mich. Rem: bro
    of #243
    Laura dau f #253
    Joseph F. son m #254
    George W. D. son m #255
SNAY, John 48 m #256 Res: Grand Haven, Mich. Rem: bro
    of #243 & #252
    Jennie dau 24 f #257
    Fannie dau 21 f #258
MACKEY, Peter 65 m #259 Res: Bradley, Mich.
NAW-ZHEE-WAY-QUAY, Sarah 53 f #260 Res: Hamilton,
    Mich.
    Mary dau f #261
    Jacob son m #262
AS-SIG-IN-AC, Angeline 52 f #263 Res: 232 Pearl St.,
    Benton Harbor, Mich. Rem: wife of Louis, not
    on roll
    Mitchell son 34 m #264 Res: Benton Harbor, Mich.
    Lucy dau 31 f #265 Res: Benton Harbor, Mich.
    William son 19 m #266 Res: 232 Pearl St., Benton
    Harbor, Mich.
    Frank son 15 m #267
WALKER, George 41 m #268 Res: Beal City, Mich. Rem:
    son of #12; not named & included on schedule
    A, see below

The name of George Walker does not appear on
schedule "A" from which it was undoubtedly omitted
through error or oversight. His right to be included
therein as a son of Betsey Walker was duly proved by
competent testimony (see evidence of David K. Foster
as given at Bradley, Mich. Dec 19th 1899 on page 66 of
report of Court of Claims; also that of Isaac Kay-kake
on page 75, and that of Charles Hickey on page 81 of
same report. There is no objection by way of the
beneficiaries herein named to the fact that the
attested copy of "Findings IV" and of schedule "A" as
printed & attached thereto that two hundred & seventy
two (272) are recited in said schedule amd of these,
three (3) viz. Mary, Lucy & Elizabeth Wezoo are
duplicated leaving but 269 persons represented by said
schedule "A" unless other names should be found to
take the place of said duplicates. If the exact
wording of the appropriation Act of April 21st 04 (33

stats 210) cuts No. 268 out, there are but 267 found and known as entitled to payment of the sum provided viz. $78,329.25, which divided -- If for 267, each share will be $293.36+ deducting 25% as agreed upon with Judge Shipman leaves the amount to be paid each share $220.02+ or if for 268 each share will be $292.23+ deducting 25% as agreed upon with Judge Shipman leaves the amount to be paid each share $219.20+.

We Phineas Pamp-to-pe and Samuel Mendokay the undersigned both Pottawatomie Indians of the State of Michigan certify that we are well acquainted with all the persons named in the foregoing schedule as numbered from 1 to 268 inclusive and that the facts set forth in said schedule are correct & true; that the persons therein named are the identical persons named and otherwise specified in said schedule "A" as the lawful beneficiaries of a claim as passed upon & issued by the Court of Claims No 21300 in case of Phineas Pamp-to-pe Etal V. The United States; and we further certify that the places of residence of those now living together with those of administrators and guardians duly appointed for the deceased and minors, as stated herein to be their present Post Office addresses to the best of our knowledge and belief, & we further certify that we have read this schedule and the affidavit as herein made and understand fully the contents thereof and we further declare aur disinterestedness in this matter except as we and individually concerned, and it is our further belief that George Walker No 268 on this schedule should be included in the payment of the claim.

Phineas Pamp te pe
Samuel Mendokay

Subscribed & sworn to before me at Coldwater Mich this 21st day of October 1904

S. L. Taggart Spl US Ind Agt

I certify the foregoing schedule to be correct and with exception of the addition of George Walker and the elimination of the duplicated names of Mary, Lucy & Elizabeth Wezoo, to be the identical persons named & otherwise specified in schedule "A" of the Court of Claims, as the beneficiaries in the the payment of the sum of $78,329.25 to be made to the Pottawatomie Indians of the State of Michigan. Coldwater Mich

October 26th 1904
                S. L. Taggart
                Spl US Ind Agt

    Approved by the Department with exception of #268
on Nov. 11, 1904. See 79790/04 and office letter to
Special Indian Agent Samuel L. Taggart, dated Nov. 17
1904.   Letters of guardianship and administrations
filed with 76431/04.

                ————————